ZONDERVAN
Charts

D1430539

CHRONOLOGICAL AND BACKGROUND
CHARTS OF

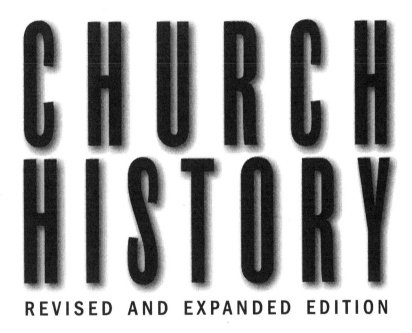

CHURCH HISTORY

REVISED AND EXPANDED EDITION

43 NEW CHARTS

Robert C. Walton

ZONDERVAN®

ZONDERVAN.com/
AUTHORTRACKER
follow your favorite authors

Books in the Zondervan*Charts* Series

Charts of Ancient and Medieval Church History (John D. Hannah)

Charts of Bible Prophecy (H. Wayne House and Randall Price)

Charts of Christian Theology and Doctrine (H. Wayne House)

Charts of Cults, Sects, and Religious Movements (H. Wayne House)

Charts of the Gospels and the Life of Christ (Robert L. Thomas)

Charts of Modern and Postmodern Church History (John D. Hannah)

Chronological and Background Charts of Church History (Robert C. Walton)

Chronological and Background Charts of the New Testament (H. Wayne House)

Chronological and Background Charts of the Old Testament (John H. Walton)

Chronological and Thematic Charts of Philosophies and Philosophers (Milton D. Hunnex)

Taxonomic Charts of Theology and Biblical Studies (M. James Sawyer)

Timeline Charts of the Western Church (Susan Lynn Peterson)

CHRONOLOGICAL AND BACKGROUND CHARTS OF

CHURCH HISTORY

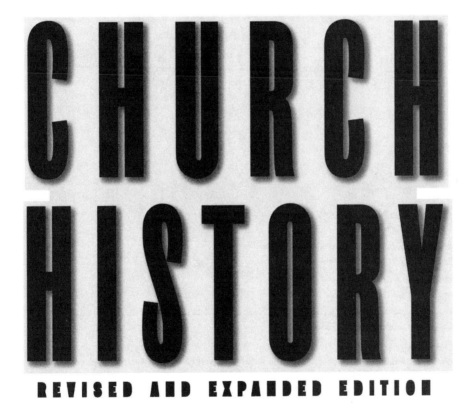

REVISED AND EXPANDED EDITION

43 NEW CHARTS

Robert C. Walton

ZONDERVAN

GRAND RAPIDS, MICHIGAN 49530 USA

 ZONDERVAN®

Chronological and Background Charts of Church History
Copyright © 1986, 2005 by Robert C. Walton

Requests for information should be addressed to:

Zondervan, *Grand Rapids, Michigan* 49530

Library of Congress Cataloging-in-Publication Data

Walton, Robert C. (Robert Charles)
    Chronological and background charts of church history / Robert C. Walton—Rev. and expanded ed.
      p. cm. - (ZondervanCharts)
    Includes bibliographical references and index.
    ISBN 978-0-310-25813-1
    1. Church history—Chronology—Charts, diagrams, etc. I. Title. II. Series.
  BR149.W25 2005
  270'.02'02—dc22

2005017303

Interior design by Angela Eberlein

Printed in the United States of America

10 11 12 13 14 15 16 17 • 15 14 13 12 11 10 9 8 7 6

To Chris

Contents

The Reformation (1517–1648)

The Modern Church (from 1648)

Foreword

This is an era when people downgrade or ignore the value of both secular and sacred history. Cicero wisely said that those who know nothing of the past before their birth are doomed to be like children living in the present without the valuable wisdom of the past. Santayana believed that those who forget or ignore the past are doomed to repeat its least desirable features.

This should not be true of those who take advantage of the charts and diagrams presented in this book. Church history, because the church has existed for almost two thousand years and because it has a global scope, includes a mass of complex data. The author presents the significant facts of the past in useful charts and diagrams so that the student can see what facts are important and what their relationship is to the story of the church. The book will be a useful supplement to classroom texts and lectures, supplying information on the who, what, when, where, and how of church history. It also will be useful to the general reader who desires a brief survey of the important data of church history.

Earle E. Cairns
Wheaton, Illinois

Preface

This collection of charts has a twofold purpose. The first purpose relates to the organization and accessibility of the factual information involved in the study of church history. As a church history teacher, I found that my greatest challenge lay in taking a vast amount of information and reducing it to some orderly form for the purpose of presenting it to my class. This book takes the process a step further, reducing what is often found in paragraph form to a series of charts. As such, I hope it will be helpful to student and teacher alike, both as a way of gaining rapid access to basic information without wading through many pages of text and as a way of providing orderly categories into which that information may be placed.

The second purpose relates to the interpretation and presentation of material. Many of these charts have developed out of my own teaching experience, and I trust they will be as useful to other teachers as they have been to me in presenting to students an interpretive overview of a particular trend or pattern or in providing a simple schema for grasping an especially knotty issue.

To the extent that the presentation of history is selective, it is also subjective. Nevertheless, I believe that my decisions concerning which people and facts to include and which to exclude have resulted in a collection of charts that will prove to be useful and enlightening to many people. I hope that this book may in some small measure stimulate not only understanding of, but also appreciation for, the study of church history, which is, after all, the chronicle of God's work in the world.

In this revised and expanded edition of *Chronological and Background Charts of Church History*, I had the opportunity to make many revisions to the first edition and to add more than forty new charts. I appreciate those helpful critics who corresponded with me over the last eighteen years and pointed out mistakes and suggested improvements. I trust you will find some of your ideas incorporated into this revised edition of the book.

Robert C. Walton

August 2004

OVERVIEW
AND
GENERAL CHARTS

A Timeline of Church History

	1 AD–200 AD	200 AD–400 AD	400 AD–600 AD	600 AD–800 AD	800 AD–1000 AD
PEOPLE	Peter (d.c.67) Paul (d.c.67) Ignatius (d.117) Polycarp (c.69–160) Justin Martyr (c.100–165) Tertullian (c.160–c.220) Origen (c.185–c.254)	Anthony of Thebes (c.251–356) Constantine (d.337) Athanasius (c.296–373) Jerome (c.345–420) Augustine of Hippo (354–430) Patrick (c.390–c.461)	Leo I (d.461) Boethius (c.480–524) Benedict of Nursia (480–c.543) Gregory I (c.540–604)	Charlemagne (742–814) Nicholas I (d.867)	
EVENTS	Pentecost (c.33) Paul's Missionary Journeys (c.46–c.57) Neronian Persecution (64) Fall of Jerusalem (70) Completion of New Testament (c.95)	Edict of Milan (313) Council of Nicea (325) Council of Constantinople (371) Christianity becomes the official religion of the Roman Empire (381)	Latin Vulgate (c.400) Augustine's *The City of God* (427) Council of Ephesus (431) Council of Chalcedon (451) Fall of Roman Empire in the West (476) Council of Orange (529)	Muslim Conquest (633–732) Iconoclastic Controversy (725–843) Donation of Pepin (752)	Charlemagne crowned Holy Roman Emperor (800) Donation of Constantine (c.800) Cluny monastery founded (910)

Chart 1

	1000 AD–1200 AD	1200 AD–1400 AD	1400 AD–1600 AD	1600 AD–1800 AD	1800 AD–2000 AD
PEOPLE	Gregory VII (c.1033–1085) Anselm (c.1033–1109) Peter Abelard (c.1079–1142) Bernard of Clairvaux (1090–1153) Richard I (1157–1199) Innocent III (1160–1216) Francis of Assisi (1182–1226)	Thomas Aquinas (1224–1274) Boniface VIII (d.1303) John Wycliffe (c.1329–1384) John Huss (1373–1415)	Savonarola (1452–1498) Desiderius Erasmus (c.1466–1536) Leo X (1475–1521) Martin Luther (1483–1546) Henry VIII (1491–1547) Ignatius Loyola (1491–1556) John Calvin (1509–1564)	John Bunyan (1628–1688) Philip Spener (1635–1705) Cotton Mather (1663–1728) Joseph Butler (1692–1752) Jonathan Edwards (1703–1791) John Wesley (1703–1791) George Whitefield (1714–1770) William Wilberforce (1759–1833) William Carey (1761–1834) Charles Finney (1792–1875) Charles Hodge (1797–1878)	William Booth (1829–1912) Dwight L. Moody (1837–1899) Abraham Kuyper (1837–1920) Albert Schweitzer (1875–1965) J. Gresham Machen (1881–1937) Karl Barth (1886–1968) Francis Schaeffer (1912–1985) Billy Graham (b.1918)
EVENTS	Great Schism (1054) Crusades (1095–1291)	Fourth Lateran Council (1215) Magna Carta (1215) Aquinas's *Summa Theologica* (1273) "Babylonian Captivity" of the Papacy (1309–1378) Great Papal Schism (1378–1417)	Council of Constance (1414–1418) Fall of Constantinople (1453) Gutenberg Bible (c.1460) Ninety-five Theses (1517) Diet of Worms (1521) Jesuits founded (1534) Council of Trent (1545–1563) Spanish Armada (1588) Edict of Nantes (1598)	King James Bible (1611) Pilgrims land (1620) Westminster Assembly (1643–1649) First Great Awakening (c.1725–c.1760)	First Vatican Council (1870) Edinburgh Conference (1910) Second Vatican Council (1962–1965)

Chart 1

The Parallel Structures of Systematic Theology and Church History

OUTLINE OF SYSTEMATIC THEOLOGY	PARALLEL DEVELOPMENTS IN CHURCH HISTORY
Bibliology – The Doctrine of Scripture	Gnosticism and the Canon of the New Testament (2nd–4th centuries)
Theology Proper – The Doctrine of God Christology – The Doctrine of Christ Pneumatology – The Doctrine of the Holy Spirit	Trinitarian Controversy (4th century) Christological Controversy (5th century)
Anthropology – The Doctrine of Man	Pelagian Controversy (5th–7th centuries)
Soteriology – The Doctrine of Salvation	The Reformation: Protestant vs. Catholic (16th century), Reformed vs. Arminian (17th century)
Ecclesiology – The Doctrine of the Church	The Reformation: Protestant vs. Catholic (16th century), Lutheran and Reformed vs. Anabaptist (16th–17th centuries)
Eschatology – The Doctrine of Last Things	Dispensationalism, Adventism, etc. (19th–20th centuries)

Chart 2

The Pendulum Effect in Church History

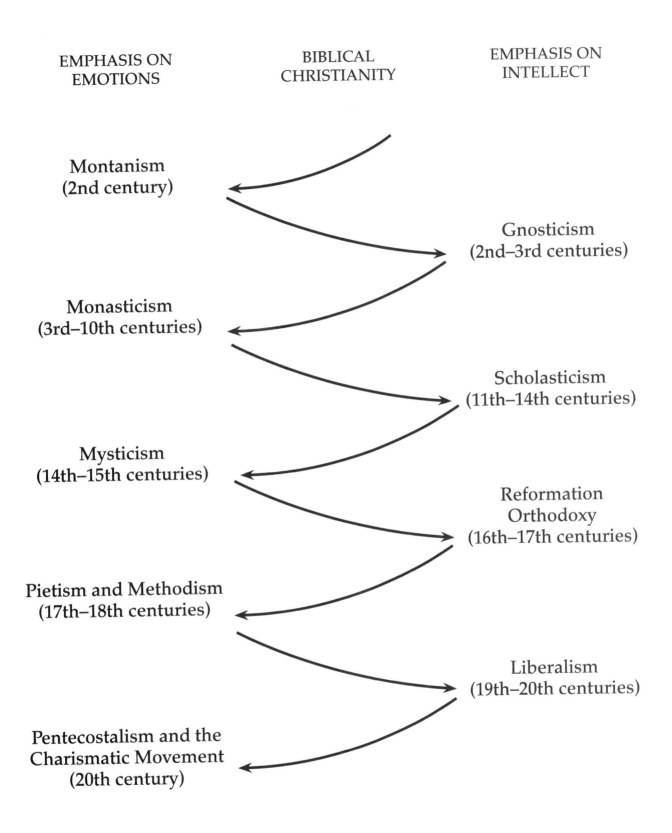

EMPHASIS ON
EMOTIONS

BIBLICAL
CHRISTIANITY

EMPHASIS ON
INTELLECT

Montanism
(2nd century)

Gnosticism
(2nd–3rd centuries)

Monasticism
(3rd–10th centuries)

Scholasticism
(11th–14th centuries)

Mysticism
(14th–15th centuries)

Reformation
Orthodoxy
(16th–17th centuries)

Pietism and Methodism
(17th–18th centuries)

Liberalism
(19th–20th centuries)

Pentecostalism and the
Charismatic Movement
(20th century)

Chart 3

Divine Sovereignty and Free Will—The Debate through the Centuries

CONTEXT	TIME	EMPHASIZING SOVEREIGNTY	COMPROMISE POSITION	EMPHASIZING FREE WILL
Pelagian Controversy	4th–6th centuries	Augustine of Hippo	John Cassian (Semi-Pelagianism) Caesarius of Arles (Semi-Augustinianism)	Pelagius
Predestination Controversy	9th century	Gottschalk	Rabanus Maurus opposed Gottschalk's view of double predestination	
Early Reformation	16th century	Luther – The Bondage of the Will		Erasmus – The Freedom of the Will
Dutch Reformed Church	17th century	Francis Gomarus and Synod of Dordt supporting Calvinism		Jacob Arminius Simon Episcopius and Remonstrants
English Baptists	17th century	Henry Jacob and the Particular Baptists		Thomas Helwys and the General Baptists
Swiss Reformed Church	17th century	Francis Turretin and the Helvetic Consensus	Moses Amyraut (Amyraldianism)	
American Congregationalism	17th–18th centuries	Jonathan Edwards Timothy Dwight	Samuel Hopkins, Nathaniel Taylor, and the New Haven Theology	
American Baptists	18th century	The Philadelphia Association and other Calvinistic Baptists		Paul Palmer and the Free Will Baptists
Methodist Revival	18th century	George Whitefield and the Calvinistic Methodists		John Wesley and the Methodist Church
American Presbyterians	19th century	Presbyterian Church in the USA supported Westminster Standards	Cumberland Presbyterian Church rejected predestination	
Downgrade Controversy	19th century	Charles Haddon Spurgeon and other English Baptists		Baptist Union accepted General Baptists and their Arminian views

Chart 4

The Popes Recognized by the Roman Catholic Church

NAME AND DATES	NAME AND DATES	NAME AND DATES	NAME AND DATES	NAME AND DATES
Peter (30–67)	Stephen III (752–757)	Gregory V (996–999)	Gregory X (1271–1276)	Innocent IX (1591)
Linus (67–76)	Paul I (757–767)	Sylvester II (999–1003)	Innocent V (1276)	Clement VIII (1592–1605)
Anacletus (76–88)	Stephen IV (768–772)	John XVII (1003)	Adrian V (1276)	Leo XI (1605)
Clement I (88–97)	Adrian I (772–795)	John XVIII (1004–1009)	John XXI (1276–1277)	Paul V (1605–1621)
Evaristus (97–105)	Leo III (795–816)	Sergius IV (1009–1012)	Nicholas III (1277–1280)	Gregory XV (1621–1623)
Alexander I (105–115)	Stephen V (816–817)	Benedict VIII (1012–1024)	Martin IV (1281–1285)	Urban VIII (1623–1644)
Sixtus I (115–125)	Paschal I (817–824)	John XIX (1024–1032)	Honorius IV (1285–1287)	Innocent X (1644–1655)
Telesphorus (125–136)	Eugene II (824–827)	Benedict IX (1032–1044)	Nicholas IV (1288–1292)	Alexander VII (1655–1667)
Hyginus (136–140)	Valentine (827)	Sylvester III (1045)	Celestine V (1294)	Clement IX (1667–1669)
Pius I (140–155)	Gregory IV (827–844)	Benedict IX (1045)	Boniface VIII (1294–1303)	Clement X (1670–1676)
Anicetus (155–166)	Sergius II (844–847)	Gregory VI (1045–1046)	Benedict XI (1303–1304)	Innocent XI (1676–1689)
Soter (166–175)	Leo IV (847–855)	Clement II (1046–1047)	Clement V (1304–1314)	Alexander VIII (1689–1691)
Eleutherius (175–189)	Benedict III (855–858)	Benedict X (1047–1048)	John XXII (1316–1334)	Innocent XII (1691–1700)
Victor I (189–199)	Nicholas I (858–867)	Damasus II (1048)	Benedict XII (1334–1342)	Clement XI (1700–1721)
Zephyrinus (199–217)	Adrian II (867–872)	Leo IX (1049–1054)	Clement VI (1342–1352)	Innocent XIII (1721–1724)
Callistus I (217–222)	John VIII (872–882)	Victor II (1055–1057)	Innocent VI (1352–1362)	Benedict XIII (1724–1730)
Urban I (222–230)	Marinus I (882–884)	Stephen X (1057–1058)	Urban V (1362–1370)	Clement XII (1730–1740)
Pontianus (230–235)	Adrian III (884–885)	Nicholas II (1059–1061)	Gregory XI (1370–1378)	Benedict XIV (1740–1758)
Anterus (235–236)	Stephen VI (885–891)	Alexander II (1061–1073)	Urban VI (1378–1389)*	Clement XIII (1758–1769)
Fabian (236–250)	Formosus (891–896)	Gregory VII (1073–1085)	Boniface IX (1389–1404)*	Clement XIV (1769–1774)
Cornelius (251–253)	Boniface VI (896)	Victor III (1086–1087)	Innocent VII (1404–1406)*	Pius VI (1775–1799)
Lucius I (253–254)	Stephen VII (896–897)	Urban II (1088–1099)	Gregory XII (1406–1415)*	Pius VII (1800–1823)
Stephen I (254–257)	Romanus (897)	Paschal II (1099–1118)	Martin V (1417–1431)	Leo XII (1823–1829)
Sixtus II (257–258)	Theodore II (897)	Gelasius II (1118–1119)	Eugene IV (1431–1447)	Pius VIII (1829–1830)
Dionysius (259–268)	John IX (898–900)	Callistus II (1119–1124)	Nicholas V (1447–1455)	Gregory XVI (1831–1846)
Felix I (269–274)	Benedict IV (900–903)	Honorius II (1124–1130)	Callistus III (1455–1458)	Pius IX (1846–1878)
Eutychianus (275–283)	Leo V (903)	Innocent II (1130–1143)	Pius II (1458–1464)	Leo XIII (1878–1903)
Caius (283–296)	Sergius III (904–911)	Celestine II (1143–1144)	Paul II (1464–1471)	Pius X (1903–1914)
Marcellinus (296–304)	Anastasius III (911–913)	Lucius II (1144–1145)	Sixtus IV (1471–1484)	Benedict XV (1914–1922)
Marcellus I (308–309)	Lando (913–914)	Eugene III (1145–1153)	Innocent VIII (1484–1492)	Pius XI (1922–1939)
Eusebius (310)	John X (914–928)	Anastasius IV (1153–1154)	Alexander VI (1492–1503)	Pius XII (1939–1958)
Melchiades (311–314)	Leo VI (928)	Adrian IV (1154–1159)	Pius III (1503)	John XXIII (1958–1963)
Sylvester I (314–335)	Stephen VIII (928–931)	Alexander III (1159–1181)	Julius II (1503–1513)	Paul VI (1963–1978)
Mark (336)	John XI (931–935)	Lucius III (1181–1185)	Leo X (1513–1521)	John Paul I (1978)
Julius I (337–352)	Leo VII (936–939)	Urban III (1185–1187)	Adrian VI (1522–1523)	John Paul II (1978–2005)
Liberius (352–366)	Stephen IX (939–942)	Gregory VIII (1187)	Clement VII (1523–1534)	Benedict XVI (2005–)
Damasus I (366–384)	Marinus II (942–946)	Clement III (1187–1191)	Paul III (1534–1549)	
Siricius (384–399)	Agapitus II (946–955)	Celestine III (1191–1198)	Julius III (1550–1555)	*For schismatic popes, see Chart 46.
Anastasius I (399–401)	John XII (955–963)	Innocent III (1198–1216)	Marcellus II (1555)	
Innocent I (401–417)	Leo VIII (963–964)	Honorius III (1216–1227)	Paul IV (1555–1559)	
Zozimus (417–418)	Benedict V (964)	Gregory IX (1227–1241)	Pius IV (1559–1565)	
Boniface I (418–422)	John XIII (965–972)	Celestine IV (1241)	Pius V (1566–1572)	
Celestine I (422–432)	Benedict VI (973–974)	Innocent IV (1243–1254)	Gregory XIII (1572–1585)	
Sixtus III (432–440)	Benedict VII (974–983)	Alexander IV (1254–1261)	Sixtus V (1585–1590)	
Leo I (440–461)	John XIV (983–984)	Urban IV (1261–1264)	Urban VII (1590)	
Hilarus (461–468)	John XV (985–996)	Clement IV (1265–1268)	Gregory XIV (1590–1591)	
Simplicius (468–483)				
Felix II (483–492)				
Gelasius I (492–496)				
Anastasius II (496–498)				
Symmachus (498–514)				
Hormisdas (514–523)				
John I (523–526)				
Felix III (526–530)				
Boniface II (530–532)				
John II (533–535)				
Agapitus I (535–536)				
Silverius (536–537)				
Vigilius (537–555)				
Pelagius I (556–561)				
John III (561–574)				
Benedict I (575–579)				
Pelagius II (579–590)				
Gregory I (590–604)				
Sabinianus (604–606)				
Boniface III (607)				
Boniface IV (608–615)				
Adeodatus I (615–618)				
Boniface V (619–625)				
Honorius I (625–638)				
Severinus (640)				
John IV (640–642)				
Theodore I (642–649)				
Martin I (649–655)				
Eugene I (655–657)				
Vitalian (657–672)				
Adeodatus II (672–676)				
Donus (676–678)				
Agatho (678–681)				
Leo II (682–683)				
Benedict II (684–685)				
John V (685–686)				
Cono (686–687)				
Sergius I (687–701)				
John VI (701–705)				
John VII (705–707)				
Sisinnius (708)				
Constantine (708–715)				
Gregory II (715–731)				
Gregory III (731–741)				
Zachary (741–752)				
Stephen II (752)				

Chart 5

Branches of Eastern Orthodox Christianity

CHURCH	ORIGIN	HISTORICAL NOTES
ALBANIAN ORTHODOX CHURCH	Albanian Christians sub-jected to Patriarch of Constantinople in 840	Long divided between loyalties to Rome and Constantinople. Suffered forced conversions under Muslim rule. Church became autocephalous in 1922. First American congregation formed in 1923.
ARMENIAN CHURCH	King Tiridates III baptized in 301 by Gregory the Illuminator	Oldest national church; Monophysite. Headed by Patriarch of Etchmiadzin; not formally united with Orthodox Church. Suffered persecution from Persians and Turks, including genocide in 1915. First American congregation formed in 1891.
BULGARIAN ORTHODOX CHURCH	Baptism of Prince Boris in 845	Church became autocephalous in early tenth century. Under jurisdiction of Constantinople 1767–1870. Headed by Patriarch of Sofia. American mission organized in 1909.
COPTIC CHURCH	Traditionally founded by Mark in the first century	Rejected Council of Chalcedon, became Monophysite. Suffered periodic persecution under Arab rule. Has long history of monasticism.
CYPRIOT CHURCH	Island originally evangelized by Paul and Barnabas (Acts 13)	Independence of church recognized at Council of Ephesus in 431. Crusader era brought struggle for control between Greek and Latin churchmen. Archbishop Makarios became first president of Cyprus in 1960.
ETHIOPIAN CHURCH	Christianity introduced by Frumentius in fourth century	Also known as Abyssinian Church. Long controlled by Monophysite Coptic Church. Has long history of practicing polygamy. Gained autocephalous standing from Coptic Church in 1959.
GEORGIAN CHURCH	Cappadocian slave woman Nina converted royal family c.330	Church became autocephalous in the eighth century. Under jurisdiction of Russian Orthodox Church 1811–1917.

Chart 6

CHURCH	ORIGIN	HISTORICAL NOTES
GREEK ORTHODOX CHURCH	Schism from Catholic Church in 1054 led by Michael Cerularius	Roots in Byzantine Empire. Patriarch of Constantinople recognized as Ecumenical Patriarch. Denies supremacy of pope; emphasizes seven Ecumenical Councils. Greek Orthodox Archdiocese of North and South America founded in 1922.
MALABAR CHRISTIANS	Region in South India traditionally evangelized by the apostle Thomas in the first century	Also known as Thomas Christians. Affiliated with Syrian Orthodox Church; Monophysite.
ROMANIAN ORTHODOX CHURCH	Church planted by Roman soldiers in the fourth century	Separated from Constantinople in 1859. Church recognized as autocephalous in 1885. Became national church of Romania in 1923. American Episcopate established in 1929.
RUSSIAN ORTHODOX CHURCH	Conversion of Prince Vladimir of Kiev in 988 by Cyril and Methodius	Church became autocephalous in 1448. Moscow became "Third Rome" with fall of Constantinople in 1453. Entered Alaska in 1792. Joined World Council of Churches in 1961. American churches divided over acceptance of authority of Moscow patriarchate.
SERBIAN ORTHODOX CHURCH	Conversion of Prince Mutimir in late ninth century	Church became autocephalous in 1219 under leadership of Sava. Under jurisdiction of Constantinople 1766–1879. Headed by patriarch of Belgrade. Diocese organized in the United States in 1921.
SYRIAN ORTHODOX CHURCH	Church founded in Antioch in the first century	Rejected Council of Chalcedon, became Monophysite. Suffered persecution at the hands of the Turks. Headed by patriarch of Damascus. Archdiocese in the United States established in 1957.
UKRAINIAN ORTHODOX CHURCH	Christianity came to Kiev around 862 with the conversion of princes Askold and Dyr	Under patriarchate of Moscow 1686–1917. Church became autocephalous in 1921. Church in the United States was established in 1919.

Chart 6

Major Styles of Church Architecture

STYLE	PERIOD	CHARACTERISTICS	EXAMPLES
EARLY CHRISTIAN	4th–8th centuries	Basilica style, containing narthex, nave, and apse; some added transept to give T-shaped or cruciform space. Initially rectangular with horizontal axis, later circular with vertical axis. Often contain domes above rectangular or octagonal supports. Decorated with mosaics.	Old St. Peter's, Rome San Vitale, Ravenna Hagia Sophia, Constantinople (Istanbul)
ROMANESQUE	9th–12th centuries	Narthex expanded into minor nave. Second transept added. Chapels extending from arms of transepts. Apse expanded, also surrounded by chapels. Nave topped by barrel vaults and pointed arches, often with towers at corners. Decorated with tapestries.	Durham Cathedral Church of La Madeleine, Vézelay
GOTHIC	12th–14th centuries	Brought together techniques developed during Romanesque period, maintaining similar internal structure. Added thinner walls, higher pointed spires, rose windows, flying buttresses. Greater use of stained glass, more windows allowing more light in interior. Decorated with paintings, reliefs, gargoyles. Cathedrals intended to be "Bibles in stone and glass."	Abbey Church of St. Denis, Paris Notre Dame, Paris Chartres Cathedral Salisbury Cathedral Westminster Abbey, London Ulm Cathedral
RENAISSANCE	15th–16th centuries	Huge cupolas roofing large inner spaces. Decorated with paintings, reliefs, free-standing statuary, stained glass.	Florence Cathedral Sistine Chapel, Rome St. Peter's Basilica, Rome San Giorgio Maggiore, Venice
BAROQUE	17th–18th centuries	Columned facades. Wide nave with small or no side aisles. Oval or circular dome over intersection of nave and transept. Illusions gave sense of expanded or even infinite space.	Il Gesù, Rome St. Paul's, London St. Martin-in-the-Fields, London
ROCOCO	18th century	Ornate, colorful decor, including sculptures and paintings of cherubs. Vertical axis.	Wieskirche, Bavaria
NEO-CLASSICAL	19th century	Imitated architectural styles of ancient Greece and Rome, thus look like pagan temples. Extensive use of columns.	La Madeleine, Paris
GOTHIC REVIVAL	19th century	Interest in Gothic associated with Romantic movement led to attempts to imitate medieval cathedrals.	Fonthill Abbey, Wiltshire St. Patrick's Cathedral, New York

Chart 7

Great Hymn Writers

NAME	DATES	CHURCH AFFILIATION	BIRTHPLACE	REPRESENTATIVE HYMNS
Clement of Alexandria	c.150–c.215	Old Catholic	Athens	*Shepherd of Tender Youth* (first extant Christian hymn)
Ambrose	340–397	Old Catholic	Gaul	*O Splendor of God's Glory Bright* *From Where the Rising Sun*
Prudentius	348–413	Roman Catholic	Saragossa, Spain	*Of the Father's Love Begotten* *Cease, Ye Tearful Mourners*
Venantius Fortunatus	c.530–c.610	Roman Catholic	Treviso, Italy	*Praise the Savior Now and Ever* *Welcome, Happy Morning*
Caedmon	7th century	Roman Catholic	Northumbria	Bible stories in verse set to music
John of Damascus	c.675–749	Eastern Orthodox	Damascus	*Come, Ye Faithful, Raise the Strain*
Bernard of Clairvaux	c.1090–1153	Roman Catholic	Fontaines, France	*Jesus, Thou Joy of Loving Hearts* *O Sacred Head, Now Wounded*
Adam of St. Victor	c.1110–1180	Roman Catholic	Paris, France	Liturgical hymns
Bernard of Cluny	12th century	Roman Catholic	Brittany	*Jerusalem, the Golden* *Brief Life Is Here Our Portion*
Martin Luther	1483–1546	Lutheran	Eisleben, Germany	*A Mighty Fortress Is Our God* *From the Depths of Woe*
Paul Gerhardt	c.1607–1676	Lutheran	Wittenberg, Germany	*All My Heart This Night Rejoices* *Why Should Cross and Trial Grieve Me?*
Thomas Ken	1637–1711	Anglican	Hertfordshire, England	*Praise God from Whom All Blessings Flow* *All Praise to Thee, My God, This Night*
Joachim Neander	1650–1680	German Reformed	Bremen, Germany	*Praise Ye the Lord, the Almighty* *Wondrous King, All Glorious*
Joseph Addison	1672–1719	Anglican	Amesbury, England	*The Spacious Firmament on High* *When All Thy Mercies, O My God*
Isaac Watts	1674–1748	Congregation-alist	Southampton, England	*When I Survey the Wondrous Cross* *Jesus Shall Reign* (and about 600 others)
Gerhard Tersteegen	1697–1769	German Reformed	Prussia	*God Himself Is with Us* *God Calling Yet! Shall I Not Hear*
Nikolaus von Zinzendorf	1700–1760	Moravian	Dresden, Germany	*Jesus, Thy Blood and Righteousness* *Jesus, Lead Thou On*
Philip Doddridge	1702–1751	Congregation-alist	London, England	*O Happy Day* *Grace! 'Tis a Charming Sound*
Charles Wesley	1708–1788	Anglican	Epworth, England	*Hark, the Herald Angels Sing* *O, For a Thousand Tongues* (and about 6,000 others)
John Newton	1725–1807	Anglican	London, England	*Amazing Grace* *Glorious Things of Thee Are Spoken*
William Cowper	1731–1800	Anglican	Hertfordshire, England	*There Is a Fountain Filled with Blood* *God Moves in a Mysterious Way*
Augustus Toplady	1740–1778	Anglican	Surrey, England	*Rock of Ages* *A Debtor to Mercy Alone*
James Montgomery	1771–1854	Moravian	Ayrshire, Scotland	*Angels from the Realms of Glory* *In the Hour of Trial*

Chart 8

Great Hymn Writers (continued)

NAME	DATES	CHURCH AFFILIATION	BIRTHPLACE	REPRESENTATIVE HYMNS
Reginald Heber	1783–1826	Anglican	Cheshire, England	*Holy, Holy, Holy* *The Son of God Goes Forth to War*
John Keble	1792–1866	Anglican	Gloucestershire, England	*Sun of My Soul, Thou Savior Dear* *God, the Lord, A King Remaineth*
George W. Doane	1799–1859	Episcopal	Trenton, NJ	*Fling Out the Banner, Let It Float* *Thou Art the Way*
Ray Palmer	1808–1887	Congregation-alist	Little Compton, RI	*My Faith Looks Up to Thee* *Take Me, O My Father, Take Me*
Horatius Bonar	1808–1889	Presbyterian	Edinburgh, Scotland	*I Heard the Voice of Jesus Say* *Thy Works, Not Mine, O Christ*
Frederick W. Faber	1814–1863	Roman Catholic	Yorkshire, England	*Faith of Our Fathers* *There's a Wideness in God's Mercy*
Edward Caswall	1814–1887	Roman Catholic	Hampshire, England	*When Morning Gilds the Skies* *See, Amid the Winter's Snow*
Fanny Crosby	1820–1915	Episcopal	Southeast, NY	*Blessed Assurance* *To God Be the Glory* (and about 2,000 others)
Cecil F. Alexander	c.1823–1895	Church of Ireland	Dublin, Ireland	*Once in Royal David's City* *There Is a Green Hill Far Away*
William W. How	1823–1897	Anglican	Shropshire, England	*For All the Saints Who from Their Labor Rest* *O Word of God Incarnate*
Robert Lowry	1826–1899	Baptist	Philadelphia, PA	*Up from the Grave He Arose* *Nothing But the Blood of Jesus*
Elizabeth C. Clephane	1830–1869	Church of Scotland	Edinburgh, Scotland	*There Were Ninety and Nine* *Beneath the Cross of Jesus*
Carolina Sandell Berg	1832–1903	Lutheran	Sweden	*Children of the Heavenly Father* *Day by Day, and With Each Passing Moment*
Frances R. Havergal	1836–1879	Anglican	Worcestershire, England	*Take My Life and Let It Be* *Who Is on the Lord's Side?*
Philip P. Bliss	1838–1876	Nondenomina-tional	Rome, PA	*Hallelujah, What a Savior* *I Will Sing of My Redeemer*
Elisha Hoffman	1839–1929	Presbyterian	Orwigsburg, PA	*What a Wonderful Savior* *Are You Washed in the Blood?*
Daniel W. Whittle	1840–1901	Nondenomina-tional	Chicopee Falls, MA	*I Know Whom I Have Believed* *Showers of Blessing*
George Matheson	1842–1906	Church of Scotland	Glasgow, Scotland	*O Love That Will Not Let Me Go* *Make Me a Captive, Lord*
J. Wilbur Chapman	1859–1918	Presbyterian	Richmond, IN	*One Day* *Jesus, What a Friend for Sinners*
Thomas O. Chisholm	1866–1960	Methodist	Franklin, KY	*Great Is Thy Faithfulness* *Living for Jesus*
Haldor Lillenas	1885–1959	Church of the Nazarene	Norway	*Wonderful Grace of Jesus* *The Bible Stands Like a Rock Undaunted*
Oswald J. Smith	1890–1986	Nondenomina-tional	Ontario, Canada	*Saved, Saved, Saved* *There Is Joy in Serving Jesus*
Margaret Clarkson	b.1915	Presbyterian	Saskatchewan, Canada	*So Send I You* *Our God Is Mighty, Worthy of All Praising*
John W. Peterson	b.1921	Nondenomina-tional	Lindsborg, KS	*Surely Goodness and Mercy* *Coming Again*

Chart 8

THE
ANCIENT CHURCH
(TO 476)

A Timeline of the Ancient Church (30–476)

	1 AD–100 AD	100 AD–200 AD	200 AD–300 AD	300 AD–400 AD	400 AD–500 AD
PEOPLE	Peter (d.c.67) Paul (d.c.67) John (d.c.100) Clement of Rome (d.c.100) Ignatius (d.c.117) Papias (c.60–c.130) Polycarp (c.69–160)	Hermas (early 2nd century) Marcion (d.c.160) Montanus (late 2nd century) Irenaeus (late 2nd century) Clement of Alexandria (c.150–215) Tertullian (c.160–c.220) Origen (c.185–c.254)	Cyprian (c.200–258) Mani (215–277) Arius (c.250–c.336) Anthony of Thebes (c.251–356) Constantine (d.337) Eusebius (c.263–c.339) Pachomius (c.290–c.346) Athanasius (c.296–373)	Apollinarius (c.310–c.390) Basil the Great (c.329–379) Martin of Tours (c.335–c.400) Ambrose (c.340–397) Jerome (c.345–420) John Chrysostom (c.347–407) Augustine (354–430) John Cassian (c.360–435) Cyril (376–444) Eutyches (c.378–454) Simeon Stylites (c.390–459) Patrick (c.390–c.461)	Pelagius (early 5th century) Nestorius (d.c.451) Leo I (d.c.461)
PERSECUTING EMPERORS	Nero (reigned 54–68) Domitian (81–96) Trajan (98–117)	Hadrian (117–138) Antoninus Pius (138–161) Marcus Aurelius (161–180) Septimus Severus (193–211)	Maximinus Thrax (235–236) Decius (249–251) Valerian (254–260) Aurelian (270–275) Diocletian (284–304)		
EVENTS	Pentecost (c.33) Paul's missionary journeys (c.46–c.57) Burning of Rome (64) Era of Roman Persecutions (64–313) Fall of Jerusalem (70) Completion of New Testament (c.95)	Muratorian Canon (c.180) Quartodeciman Controversy (189)		Edict of Milan (313) Council of Nicea (325) Ulfilas converts the Goths (c.340) Athanasius's Easter letter lists New Testament canon (367) Council of Constantinople (381) Christianity becomes official religion of Roman Empire (381)	Latin Vulgate (c.400) Alaric sacks Rome (410) Augustine's *The City of God* (427) Council of Ephesus (431) Council of Chalcedon (451) Vandals sack Rome (455) Fall of Roman Empire in the West (476)

Chart 9

The Twelve Disciples and Paul after the Death of Jesus

NAME	BIBLICAL INFORMATION	TRADITIONAL INFORMATION
SIMON PETER	Preached sermon on day of Pentecost. Healed lame man at temple gate. Withstood persecution of Sanhedrin. Rebuked Ananias and Sapphira and Simon Magus. Raised Dorcas from the dead. Preached the gospel to Cornelius. Miraculously delivered from prison. Rebuked by Paul at Antioch. Wrote two New Testament epistles.	Late traditions speak of visits to Britain and Gaul. Was crucified upside down in Rome during Neronian persecution (AD 64–68).
ANDREW		Is supposed to have preached in Scythia, Asia Minor, and Greece. Was crucified at Patras in Achaia.
JAMES, SON OF ZEBEDEE	Was executed by Herod Agrippa I.	
JOHN	Participated in healing of a lame man at the temple. Followed up Philip's work in Samaria. Was exiled late in life to the island of Patmos. Wrote a gospel, three epistles, and Apocalypse.	Ministered at Ephesus. Is said to have rebuked early Gnostic Cerinthus. Died a natural death in Ephesus c. AD 100.
PHILIP		Is said to have been crucified in Hierapolis in Asia Minor.
MATTHEW	Wrote the gospel that bears his name.	Conflicting traditions place him in Ethiopia, Parthia, Persia, and Macedonia.
THOMAS		Supposedly preached in Babylon. Strong early tradition tells of his founding churches in India and eventually being martyred there.
BARTHOLOMEW		Is supposed to have accompanied Philip to Hierapolis. Was martyred after ministry in Armenia.
JAMES, SON OF ALPHAEUS		Has been persistently confused with James the brother of Jesus in early church tradition. Possibly ministered in Syria.
THADDAEUS		Has often been confused with Jude the brother of Jesus. Tradition associates his ministry with Edessa (Mesopotamia).
SIMON THE ZEALOT		Variously (and dubiously) associated with Persia, Egypt, Carthage, and Britain.
JUDAS ISCARIOT	Hanged himself after betraying Jesus.	
PAUL	Pharisee who persecuted the church. Converted on road to Damascus. Went on three missionary journeys, preaching and founding churches. Arrested and taken to Rome. Wrote thirteen New Testament epistles.	Thought to have been freed from first Roman imprisonment and traveled to Gaul and Spain. Beheaded in Rome during Neronian persecution (AD 64–68).

Chart 10

Early Symbols of Christianity

NAME AND SYMBOL	SIGNIFICANCE
ALPHA–OMEGA	Eternality of Christ (see Revelation 1:8)
ANCHOR	Hope (see Hebrews 6:19)
BREAD AND WINE	Eucharist – Death of Christ
CHI–RHO	First two letters of "Christ" (ΧΡΙΣΤΟΣ) in Greek superimposed
CROSS	Death of Christ
DOVE	Holy Spirit as manifested at the baptism of Christ
FIRE	Holy Spirit on day of Pentecost
FISH	Initial letters of "Jesus Christ, God's Son, Savior" in Greek, spelling ICHTHUS (ΙΧΘΥΣ), the Greek word for "fish"; feeding of 5,000, "fishers of men"
IC XC NIKA	Symbol of Christ the Conqueror, consisting of the first and last letters of the Greek words for "Jesus" (ΙΗΣΟΥΣ) and "Christ" (ΧΡΙΣΤΟΣ) and the Latin for "Victory" (NIKA) around a cross
IHS (sometimes IHC)	First three letters of "Jesus" (ΙΗΣΟΥΣ) in Greek
INRI	Initial letters of inscription on Christ's cross in Latin – *Iesus Nazarenus Rex Iudaeorum* (Jesus of Nazareth, King of the Jews; see John 19:19)
LAMB	Christ's self-sacrifice
PALM BRANCH	Christ's triumphal entry; also associated with martyrdom
PHOENIX	A legendary bird that burns itself on a funeral pyre then comes back to life; it was used as early as the writings of Clement of Rome as a symbol of the Resurrection
SHEPHERD	Christ's care for his people
SHIP	Church (Noah's ark; cf. baptism, 1 Peter 3:20–21)
VINE	Christ's union with his people; wine of Eucharist

Chart 11

Worship in the Early Church

OBSERVANCE	TIME	PRACTICE	HISTORICAL NOTES
SABBATH	Weekly	Singing, Scripture reading, exhortation, prayer, Communion.	Adapted from Jewish synagogue service. Moved to Sunday to commemorate Christ's resurrection. Sunday declared a legal holiday under Constantine.
BAPTISM	As needed	Immersion of believers initially, though mode considered flexible. During 2nd century, baptisms often occurred on Easter Sunday after a period of catechesis and fasting. Followed by anointing with oil to represent the Holy Spirit. Infant baptism gained prevalence after Edict of Milan.	Commanded by Christ in the New Testament. Mode altered because of persecutions, climate, and later to accommodate baptism of infants. Infant baptism often accompanied by belief in baptismal regeneration.
EUCHARIST	Weekly	Common loaf and common cup shared by congregants at end of service. Accompanied by holy kiss. Initially accompanied by communal "love feast."	Commanded by Christ in the New Testament. Source of charge of cannibalism against early Christians. Generally closed to nonmembers. As church leaders came to be thought of as priests, Eucharist came to be described as sacrifice. Language used to describe Eucharist in this period contains elements of both representation and Real Presence.
EASTER	Annually	Observance of the death and resurrection of Christ. Easter preceded in early days by 40-hour fast to commemorate Christ's time in the tomb and identify with catechumens who were preparing for baptism.	First appears in the 2nd century. Quartodeciman Controversy (189) over date of observance— should it be on the day of the Jewish Passover, the 14th of Nisan—or the following Sunday? Finally observed on first Sunday after first full moon after vernal equinox. Symbols such as eggs and rabbits derived from pagan fertility rites after conversion of barbarian tribes.
LENT	Annually	Abstinence before Easter later expanded to 40-day partial fast and time of penitence.	First mentioned in writings of Council of Nicea in 325. Also associated with the temptation of Christ in the wilderness.

Chart 12

Worship in the Early Church (continued)

OBSERVANCE	TIME	PRACTICE	HISTORICAL NOTES
ASCENSION	Annually	Observance of the ascension of Christ into heaven following his resurrection. Celebrated 40 days after Easter.	Observed on the sixth Thursday after Easter from the late 4th century. Often accompanied by processional to commemorate Christ's journey to the Mount of Olives.
PENTECOST	Annually	Observance of the coming of the Holy Spirit. Celebrated 50 days (seven weeks) after Easter. Along with Easter, popular time for baptisms.	First mentioned in the writings of the 4th century. Also known as Whitsunday.
CHRISTMAS	Annually	Observance of the birth of Christ. Accompanied by the giving of gifts.	Date or even time of year of Christ's birth unknown. Observance began in 4th century. Date of December 25th chosen to counter pagan Saturnalia observance of winter solstice. Armenian Church celebrates Christmas on January 6th.
EPIPHANY	Annually	Observance of the baptism of Christ. Later associated with visit of the magi.	Evidence for observance as early as the 3rd century. Celebrated on January 6th. Initially given more importance than Christmas in the East.
SAINTS' DAYS	Annually	Remembrance of the life, or more commonly death, of a significant member of the church.	Initially served as a way to remember the sacrifices of martyrs in the congregation. Later expanded to ascetics as well, with the end of the persecutions in the fourth century. (Martin of Tours, in the 5th century, was the first non-martyr to be recognized as a "saint.") Relics and pilgrimages associated with holy people and places became common after the Edict of Milan, spurred to a significant extent by Constantine's mother, Helena.

Chart 12

The Apostolic Fathers and Early Writings

NAME	DATES	PLACES OF MINISTRY	WRITINGS	NOTABLE FACTS
CLEMENT OF ROME	c.30–c.100	Rome	*I Clement*	Considered the fourth pope by Roman Catholic Church. Is perhaps mentioned in Philippians 4:3. Was martyred under Domitian. His letter stresses apostolic succession.
IGNATIUS	d.117	Antioch in Syria	*To the Ephesians* *To the Magnesians* *To the Trallians* *To the Romans* *To the Philadelphians* *To the Smyrnaeans* *To Polycarp*	His letters were written en route to martyrdom in Rome—a fate he joyfully espoused. Was the first to distinguish between bishops and elders. Opposed Gnostic heresies. Was martyred under Trajan.
HERMAS	Late 1st–early 2nd century	Rome	*The Shepherd*	Was a contemporary of Clement. Wrote of visions and parables. Was perhaps a former slave. Was probably Jewish.
BARNABAS OF ALEXANDRIA	Late 1st–early 2nd century	Alexandria	*Epistle of Barnabas*	Was probably an Alexandrian Jew. Was familiar with allegorical methods of Philo.
PAPIAS	c.60–c.130	Hierapolis	*Exposition of the Oracles of Our Lord*	Was an acquaintance of the apostle John. Held a premillennial view of eschatology. Claimed Mark's gospel was based on Peter's words. Said that Matthew's gospel was originally written in Aramaic.
POLYCARP	c.69–160	Smyrna	*Epistle to the Philippians*	Was an acquaintance of the apostle John. Compiled and preserved the epistles of Ignatius. Is said to have confronted Marcion as "the firstborn of Satan." Was martyred under Antoninus Pius.
Unknown author	Early 2nd century	Syria	*Didache*	Early manual of church practice. Contrasts way of life and way of death. Gives instruction for fasting, baptism, Lord's Supper. Tells how to recognize false prophets. Considered by some for inclusion in New Testament canon.

Chart 13

The Second-Century Apologists

NAME	DATES	PLACES OF MINISTRY	REPRESENTATIVE WRITINGS (* = Lost)	NOTABLE FACTS
QUADRATUS	Early 2nd century	Athens	Apology*	Was bishop of Athens. His Apology was addressed to Emperor Hadrian. Contrasts Christianity with Jewish and pagan worship.
ARISTIDES	Early 2nd century	Athens	Apology*	His Apology was addressed to Emperor Hadrian. Shows strong Pauline influence.
JUSTIN MARTYR	c.100–165	Palestine Ephesus Rome	First Apology Second Apology Dialogue with Trypho the Jew Against Heresies* Against Marcion*	Was trained in philosophy. Was an itinerant lay teacher. Personally opposed Marcion. Developed concept of logos spermaticos. Argued for Christianity on the basis of prophecy, miracles, and ethics. Was beheaded in Rome.
TATIAN	110–172	Assyria Syria Rome	Diatessaron To the Greeks	Was a pupil of Justin. Argued temporal priority of Christianity over other religions. Produced first harmony of the Gospels. Later fell into Gnosticism. His followers were called Encratites.
ATHENAGORAS	2nd century	Athens	Apology On the Resurrection of the Dead	Was a Platonist. Wrote in classical style.
THEOPHILUS	d.181	Antioch	To Autolycus	Was a severe polemicist against pagan philosophers. Was bishop of Antioch.
MELITO	d.190	Sardis	On the Passion other surviving fragments	Was bishop of Sardis. Supported Quartodecimans. Produced first Christian list of the books of the Old Testament.
HEGESIPPUS	2nd century	Syria Greece Rome	Memorials*	Was a converted Jew. Collected information on early history of the church to prove its purity and apostolicity. Blamed all heresies on Judaism.
Unknown author	Late 2nd century	Unknown	Epistle to Diognetus	Never mentioned in other ancient or medieval literature. Deals with superiority of Christianity to paganism and centrality of Christian charity. Responds to argument that Christianity was a relative newcomer on the religious scene.

Chart 14

The Arguments of the Apologists

JEWISH ARGUMENTS VS. CHRISTIANITY	RESPONSES OF APOLOGISTS
Christianity is a deviant form of Judaism.	The Jewish law is by nature temporary and points to the New Covenant.
The humble carpenter who died on a cross does not correspond to the Messiah prophesied in the Old Testament.	The Old Testament predicted both the sufferings and the glory of the Messiah.
The deity of Christ contradicts the unity of God.	The Old Testament indicates a plurality of persons within the unity of the Godhead.

APOLOGISTS' ARGUMENTS AGAINST JUDAISM
Old Testament prophecy is fulfilled in Christ. Old Testament types point to Christ. The destruction of Jerusalem showed God's condemnation of Judaism and vindication of Christianity.

PAGAN ARGUMENTS VS. CHRISTIANITY	RESPONSES OF APOLOGISTS
The doctrine of the resurrection is absurd.	There were eyewitnesses in the Gospels. The effect on the disciples was profound. There are analogies in natural cycles (e.g., seasons).
There are contradictions in the Scriptures.	Harmonies like Tatian's *Diatessaron* answer contradictions.
Atheism is widely held.	Even Plato favored an unseen god.
Christianity is the worship of a criminal.	Jesus' trial violated both Jewish and Roman law.
Christianity is a novelty.	Christianity had been in preparation for all eternity. Moses antedated pagan philosophers.
Christianity evidences a lack of patriotism.	Christians obey all laws that do not violate conscience.
Christians practice incest and cannibalism.	Observe the lifestyles of Christians, particularly the examples of the martyrs; practices of "holy kiss," Lord's Supper.
Christianity leads to the destruction of society.	Natural calamities are really the true God's judgment against false worship.

APOLOGISTS' ARGUMENTS AGAINST PAGANISM
Pagan philosophers plagiarized, stealing their best ideas from Moses and the prophets. Polytheism is a philosophical absurdity and a moral disaster. Pagan philosophers contradict one another and even themselves.

APOLOGISTS' ARGUMENTS FOR CHRISTIANITY
All truth found in pagan philosophers anticipates Christianity and is brought together by it. Miracles performed by Christ, the apostles, and other Christians prove the truth of Christianity. The spread of Christianity despite overwhelming obstacles shows it to be true. Christianity alone is suited to meet the deepest needs of human beings.

Chart 15

The Third-Century Church Fathers

NAME	DATES	PLACES OF MINISTRY	REPRESENTATIVE WRITINGS (* = Lost)	NOTABLE FACTS
IRENAEUS	Late 2nd century	Smyrna Gaul	*Against Heresies* *On the Unity of the Godhead and the Origin of Evil*	Studied under Polycarp. Was a missionary and apologist. Strong opponent of Gnosticism. Had premillennial views. Was bishop of Lyons, where he was allegedly martyred. Promoted the Rule of Faith.
CLEMENT	c.150–c.215	Alexandria Antioch Jerusalem	*Exhortation to the Greeks* *The Pedagogue* *Stromata*	Was trained in philosophy. Was converted as an adult. Emphasized Logos. Approached Scripture allegorically. Wrote oldest extant Christian hymn, *Shepherd of Tender Youth.*
TERTULLIAN	c.160–c.220	Carthage	*Prescription of Heretics* *Against Marcion* *Against Praxeus*	Was a son of a Roman army officer. Was trained in law. Was converted in middle age. Joined Montanists c.200. Laid important groundwork for doctrine of the Trinity.
JULIUS AFRICANUS	c.160–c.240	Palestine	*Chronography*	Studied under Origen. His historical research covered period from Creation to AD 221.
HIPPOLYTUS	c.170–c.236	Rome	*Philosophumena* *Numerous lost commentaries*	Studied under Irenaeus. Opposed contemporary bishops of Rome. Used allegorical method of interpretation. Died in exile in Sardinia.

Chart 16

NAME	DATES	PLACES OF MINIS-TRY	REPRESENTATIVE WRITINGS (* = Lost)	NOTABLE FACTS
ORIGEN	c.185–c.254	Alexandria Caesarea	*Hexapla* *Against Celsus* *De Principiis*	His father Leonidas was martyred in 202. Studied under Clement. Succeeded Clement as catechist in 203. Was a notable advocate of allegorical interpretation of Scripture. Taught subordination of the Son to the Father. Was extremely ascetic. Was exiled by his enemies in the church. Died after torture at the hands of the Romans.
MINUCIUS FELIX	Early 3rd century	North Africa	*Octavius*	Wrote dialogue between Christian Octavius and pagan Caecilius. Content similar to Tertullian's Apology.
CYPRIAN	c.200–258	Carthage	*Unity of the Church* *De Lapsis*	Was trained in rhetoric. Was converted in 245. Was bishop of Carthage from 248 until his death. Was influenced by Tertullian. Emphasized authority of the episcopate. Took moderate stand against those who faltered under persecution, opposing the strict view of Novatian. Was martyred under Valerian.
GREGORY THAUMATUR-GOS	c.213–270	Palestine Asia Minor	*Declaration of Faith* *Eulogy on Origen*	Was converted by and studied under Origen. Was known as the Wonder-Worker. Was bishop of Neo-Caesarea.

Chart 16

The Development of the New Testament Canon

PERIOD	CHARACTERISTICS	APPROXIMATE DATES	SIGNIFICANT SOURCES	BOOKS RECEIVED	BOOKS QUESTIONED
APOSTOLIC FATHERS	No serious debate, no official pronouncements	100–140	Quotations in Apostolic Fathers	Four Gospels Pauline Epistles (unspecified corpus)	None
GNOSTIC OPPOSITION	Reaction against Gnostic truncation of canon (esp. writings of Marcion)	140–220	Quotations in Church Fathers Muratorian Canon (c.180) Gospel of Truth (Gnostic)	Four Gospels, Acts 13 Pauline Epistles 1 Peter 1 John Jude Revelation	Hebrews, James 2 Peter 2–3 John Shepherd, Didache, Apocalypse of Peter
FINAL SOLIDIFICATION	General agreement by end of 4th century	220–400	Origen	Four Gospels, Acts 13 Pauline Epistles 1 Peter 1 John Revelation	Hebrews, James 2 Peter 2–3 John Jude Shepherd, Didache
			Eusebius	Four Gospels, Acts 14 Pauline Epistles 1 Peter 1 John	James 2 Peter 2–3 John Jude, Revelation Shepherd, Didache
			Athanasius (Paschal letter of 367 – final acceptance in the East)	Present Canon	
			Synod of Rome (382 – final acceptance in the West)	Present Canon	
			Synod of Carthage (397 – acceptance by entire church)	Present Canon	

Chart 17

Books Debated for Inclusion in the New Testament Canon

QUESTIONED BOOK	REASONS GIVEN FOR ACCEPTANCE	REASONS GIVEN FOR EXCLUSION	RESULT
HEBREWS	Thought Pauline in the East	Thought non-Pauline forgery in the West	Accepted
JAMES	Thought genuine in the East	Authorship questioned in the West	Accepted
2 PETER	Petrine authorship	Authorship questioned Similarity of chapter 2 to Jude	Accepted
2–3 JOHN	Johannine authorship	Lack of citations in early writings	Accepted
JUDE	Early citations Apostolic authorship	Authorship questioned	Accepted
REVELATION	Widely recognized as Johannine	Questioned by Eusebius largely because of his opposition to chiliasm	Accepted
THE SHEPHERD OF HERMAS	Edifying contents Vision from God	Non-apostolic origin Late date	Excluded
DIDACHE	Record of genuine apostolic traditions	Uncertain origin Late date	Excluded
APOCALYPSE OF PETER	Suspected Petrine authorship Similarity to Johannine Apocalypse	Authenticity doubted	Excluded

Chart 18

Ante-Nicene Heresies

HERESY	LEADING TEACHERS	HISTORICAL INFORMATION	CHARACTERISTIC TEACHINGS
EBIONISM (Elkesaites, Mandaeans)		Originated in Palestine in the late 1st century, later spread to Asia Minor. Was made up mostly of Jewish Christians. Used gospel of Matthew in Hebrew.	Taught universality of Mosaic law (needed for salvation). Advocated antipathy to Paul. Jesus acknowledged as the Messiah, but only as a man on whom the Spirit came at his baptism. Looked for imminent Millennium.
GNOSTICISM	Simon Magus (1st century) Cerinthus (late 1st century) Basilides (early 2nd century) Saturninus (early 2nd century) Marcion (d.c.160) Valentinus (d.c.160) Tatian (110–172)	Had roots in pagan philosophy, especially Platonism. Was influenced by Oriental mysticism. Had little appeal to the masses; most influential among church leaders. Appeared throughout Empire. Worship ranged from very simple to very elaborate. Forced church to formulate Rule of Faith and New Testament canon. Caused church to emphasize apostolic succession as repository of truth.	Thought themselves possessors of unique higher insight (gnosis). Thought themselves to be of spirit, other people of soul or body. Taught matter is evil. Held to hierarchy of aeons (Pleroma). Produced either sensuality or asceticism. Were dualistic. Generally rejected Old Testament and Judaism. Used allegorical interpretation. Said that the world was created by Demiurge (=Jehovah). Believed Christ's body was an illusion.
MONTANISM	Montanus (2nd century) Priscilla (2nd century) Maximilla (2nd century) Tertullian (c.160–c.220)	Originated in Phrygia. Later spread to Rome and North Africa.	Were ascetic. Were chiliastic. Expected imminent start of Millennium. Practiced glossolalia. Were generally orthodox in doctrine. Thought themselves to be spiritual, others carnal. Continued prophetic revelation. Held to universal priesthood of believers. Opposed art of any kind. Sought martyrdom.
MANICHAEISM	Mani (215–277)	Originated in Persia. Contains many elements of Zoroastrianism. Mani was flayed alive, his skin stuffed and hung over city gate in Persia. Augustine was a follower early in life. Similar to later Paulicians, Bogomils, Cathari, Albigensians. Was characterized by strict hierarchical organization.	Held dualistic view of creation (light vs. darkness). Believed Christ was representative of light, Satan of darkness. Said that the apostles corrupted Christ's teaching, Mani revealed it in pure form. Taught that Christ's body was illusory. Followers were severely ascetic.
NOVATIANISM	Novatian (d.c.257)	Originated after Decian persecution in North Africa. Novatian elected pope by strict party who opposed appointment of Cornelius as bishop of Rome. Novatian martyred under Valerian.	Novatian theologically orthodox, wrote fine work on the Trinity. Opposed allowing those who had lapsed during the persecution to return to the church. Condemned as schismatic, not heretical.

Chart 19

Roman Persecutions of Christians

DATES	EMPEROR	NATURE AND EXTENT OF PERSECUTION	NOTABLE MARTYRS
64	Nero	Took place in Rome and vicinity only. Christians were made scapegoats for burning Rome. Sadistic measures included burning Christians alive to illuminate Nero's gardens.	Paul Peter
c.90–96	Domitian	Capricious, sporadic, centered in Rome and Asia Minor. Christians persecuted for refusal to offer incense to genius of emperor.	Clement of Rome John (exiled to Patmos)
98–117	Trajan	Sporadically enforced. Christians were lumped with other groups whose patriotism was considered suspect. Christians were to be executed when found, but not sought out.	Ignatius Symeon Zozimus Rufus
117–138	Hadrian	Sporadically enforced. Continued policies of Trajan. Any who brought false witness against Christians were to be punished.	Telesphorus
138–161	Antoninus Pius	Sporadically enforced. Continued policies of Trajan and Hadrian.	Polycarp
161–180	Marcus Aurelius	Emperor was Stoic who opposed Christianity on philosophical grounds. Christians blamed for natural disasters.	Justin Martyr Pothinus Blandina
202–211	Septimus Severus	Conversion to Christianity forbidden.	Leonidas Irenaeus Perpetua
235–236	Maximinus the Thracian	Christian clergy ordered executed. Christians opposed because they had supported emperor's predecessor, whom he had assassinated.	Ursula Hippolytus
249–251	Decius	First empire-wide persecution. Offering of incense to genius of emperor demanded. Enthusiastic return to paganism required utter extermination of Christianity. Led to rise of Novatianism.	Fabianus Alexander of Jerusalem
257–260	Valerian	Christians' property confiscated. Christians' right of assembly prohibited.	Origen Cyprian Sixtus II
274	Aurelian	Required sun worship as official state religion, but died before it could be implemented.	
303–311	Diocletian Galerius	Worst persecution of all. Churches destroyed, Bibles burned, civil rights of Christians suspended, sacrifice to gods required. Led to rise of Donatism.	Mauritius Alban

Chart 20

Nicene and Post-Nicene Fathers

NAME	DATES	PLACES OF MINISTRY	REPRESENTATIVE WRITINGS	NOTABLE FACTS
LACTANTIUS	c.240–320	Italy Gaul	*Divine Institutes*	Was born of pagan parents. Was converted as an adult. Served as tutor to Constantine's son.
EUSEBIUS	c.263–c.339	Caesarea	*Ecclesiastical History* *Chronicle* *Life of Constantine*	Known as Father of Church History. Taught at theological school in Caesarea. Became bishop of Caesarea, refused Antioch patriarchate. Sought compromise in Arian controversy, opposing both Arius and Athanasius. Was friend and advisor of Constantine. Held antichiliastic views.
HILARY	c.291–371	Poitiers	*On the Trinity*	Was converted late in life. Was greatest Western opponent of Arianism. Was named bishop of Poitiers in 350.
ATHANASIUS	c.296–373	Alexandria	*On the Incarnation of the Divine Word* *Orations Against the Arians* *Against Apollinarius*	Was most noted defender of Trinitarian orthodoxy. Became secretary to bishop Alexander of Alexandria. Was vocal participant in Council of Nicea. Was named patriarch of Alexandria in 328. Was exiled five times. Lived ascetic life and encouraged monasticism.
CYRIL OF JERUSALEM	c.315–386	Jerusalem	*Catecheses*	Raised in Christian family. Became bishop of Jerusalem (c.350). Opposed Arianism. Exiled twice in the midst of the Arian controversy. Opposed attempt of Jews to rebuild the temple.

Chart 21

NAME	DATES	PLACES OF MINISTRY	REPRESENTATIVE WRITINGS	NOTABLE FACTS
BASIL	c.329–379	Cappadocia	*Against Eunomius* *Rule of St. Basil*	Was raised in Christian home. Studied philosophy in Athens. Lived ascetic life, wrote monastic rule that bears his name. Became bishop of Caesarea in Cappadocia. Opposed Arianism. Founded hospital for lepers.
GREGORY OF NYSSA	c.330–c.394	Cappadocia	*Against Eunomius* *Against Apollinarius* *On the Deity of the Son and the Holy Ghost*	Was brother of Basil. Was influenced by Origen. Was an allegorist. Lived ascetic life, though he did marry. Reluctantly became bishop of Nyssa in 372. Opposed Arianism. Was first to stress distinction between substance and persons in Trinity. Participated in Council of Constantinople.
GREGORY OF NAZIANZUS	c.330–c.390	Cappadocia Constantinople	*Theological Orations*	Was son of bishop of Nazianzus. Studied with Basil in Athens. Lived ascetic life. Became bishop of Nazianzus (374), then patriarch of Constantinople (381), but quickly resigned. Opposed Arianism. Was notable orator and poet.
AMBROSE	c.340–397	Milan	*On Faith* *On the Holy Ghost* *On the Sacraments*	Was son of governor of Gaul. Prepared for civil service. Became praetor of North Italy. Was acclaimed bishop of Milan in 374 before baptism. Lived ascetic life. Opposed Arianism. Withstood Emperor Theodosius over massacre of Thessalonians. Influenced Augustine through sermons.

Chart 21

Nicene and Post-Nicene Fathers (continued)

NAME	DATES	PLACES OF MINISTRY	REPRESENTATIVE WRITINGS	NOTABLE FACTS
JEROME	c.345–420	Rome Antioch Bethlehem	*Latin Vulgate* *Catalogue of Illustrious Authors* *Numerous commentaries*	Was born into Christian family. Was educated in rhetoric. Was tireless advocate of monasticism. Spent years in desert seclusion. Was one of few Christians in his age who knew Hebrew. Became secretary to Damasus, bishop of Rome. Encouraged many Roman women toward asceticism. Lived his last 35 years in a cave in Bethlehem. His Latin Vulgate later became the official Bible of the Roman Catholic Church.
JOHN CHRYSOSTOM	c.347–407	Antioch Constantinople	*On the Priesthood* *Homilies*	Chrysostom, his nickname, means "Golden Mouth." Was greatest preacher of ancient church. Stressed ethical application in sermons. Was son of Roman officer. Studied rhetoric. Preferred monastic life. Became patriarch of Constantinople in 397. Was banished by Empress Eudoxia. Died in exile.
THEODORE OF MOPSUESTIA	c.350–428	Antioch Mopsuestia	*Commentary on the Minor Prophets* *Against the Allegorists* *Against Defenders of Original Sin*	Was father of Antiochene theology. Was a friend of Chrysostom. Abandoned monastic life to marry. Was named bishop of Mopsuestia in 392. Stressed grammatical-historical context for interpretation of Scripture. Opposed allegorical interpretation of Scripture. Was teacher of Nestorius. Was condemned by Second Council of Constantinople.

Chart 21

NAME	DATES	PLACES OF MINISTRY	REPRESENTATIVE WRITINGS	NOTABLE FACTS
AUGUSTINE	354–430	North Africa	*Confessions* *Meditations* *The City of God* *Enchiridion* *Retractationes* *The Trinity*	Was born to pagan father and Christian mother. Studied Neoplatonist philosophy at Carthage. Espoused Manichaean heresy early in life. Was converted in Milan in 386. Was influenced by Ambrose. Was named bishop of Hippo in 395. Espoused mild form of asceticism. Opposed Manichaeans, Donatists, Pelagians. Wrote first Christian philosophy of history. His work was used to support both sides of almost every medieval theological debate.
CYRIL	376–444	Alexandria	*Against Nestorius* *Against Julian the Apostate*	Was champion of Alexandrian theology. Became patriarch of Alexandria c.412. Used force and duplicity against his opponents, both Christians and others. Opposed Chrysostom, Theodore, Nestorius. Advocated veneration of Mary.
LEO I	c.400–461	Rome	*Tome*	Became bishop of Rome in 440. Opposed Pelagians, Manichaeans, Monophysites. His *Tome* played key role in Chalcedonian settlement of Christological controversy. Asserted authority over entire church; authority accepted in West.

Chart 21

Development of Episcopacy in the First Five Centuries

PERIOD	SOURCE(S)	DESCRIPTION
1st century	New Testament	Elder-bishops and deacons in each church were under the supervision of the apostles.
Early 2nd century	Ignatius	Elders and bishops differentiated. Each congregation governed by a bishop, elders, and deacons.
Late 2nd century	Irenaeus Tertullian	Diocesan bishops (i.e., a bishop now oversaw a group of congregations in a geographical area); they were thought to be successors of the apostles.
Mid 3rd century	Cyprian	Priesthood and sacrifice; elders (presbuteros) come to be seen as sacrificing priests. Primacy of bishop of Rome asserted.
Early 4th century	Council of Nicea	Metropolitan bishops (archbishops) by virtue of their location in population centers gain ascendancy over chorepiscopi (country bishops).
Late 4th century	Council of Constantinople	Special honor given to bishops of Rome, Alexandria, Antioch, Constantinople, and Jerusalem—called patriarchs. Patriarch of Constantinople given primacy next to the bishop of Rome.
Mid 5th century	Leo I Council of Chalcedon	The supremacy of Rome; Leo I claimed authority over the whole church on the basis of succession from Peter.

Chart 22

Factors Contributing to the Supremacy of the Bishop of Rome

FACTOR	RESULT
MATTHEW 16:17–19	Papal claims rest on the assertion that Peter was given authority by Jesus over the entire church. This claim was first officially recognized during the papacy of Leo I.
APOSTOLIC SUCCESSION	The teaching that the apostles passed on their authority to their successors led to the conclusion that Peter's supreme authority had been perpetuated in the bishops of Rome.
MARTYRDOM OF PETER AND PAUL	With the rise of the veneration of martyred saints, Rome gained prestige as the site of the deaths of the two principal apostles. The persecution under Nero also gave to the Roman church a special prominence by virtue of its suffering.
POPULATION OF ROME	Both the size of the city and the size of the church contributed to the authority of the bishop.
IMPERIAL CAPITAL	After the Edict of Milan, the emperors often sought advice on religious matters from the bishops of Rome.
LANGUAGE	The Latin-speaking West, led by the bishop of Rome, was often able to cut through the knotty theological dilemmas that incapacitated the Greek-speaking East, because of the lesser ability of the Latin language to express subtle shades of meaning.
LOCATION	Of the five patriarchal cities, only Rome was in the West; thus the bishop of Rome exercised authority over much more territory than did the other patriarchs.
MISSIONARY OUTREACH	The bishops of Rome, such as Gregory the Great, encouraged successful missionary work among the barbarian tribes, who then looked to Rome with great respect. The Eastern patriarchs were much less successful in evangelizing the Persians and later the Muslims.
BARBARIAN INVASIONS	The collapse of the Western Empire under the barbarian invasions left the church as the major integrating force in society—in the empire as well as among the "Christian" barbarians.
MUSLIM CONQUEST	The loss of the territories of the patriarchs of Antioch, Alexandria, and Jerusalem to Islam and the continual pressure exerted against Constantinople also increased the authority of the bishop of Rome.
LEADERSHIP	Leo I played a major role in resolving the Christological controversy. Gregory I acted to protect Rome against the Lombards, encouraged mission to England, and contributed pastoral and theological writings.

Chart 23

Major Ancient Church Doctrinal Controversies

CONTROVERSY	MAJOR HERETICAL LEADERS	MAJOR ORTHODOX LEADERS	RELEVANT COUNCILS	ACCEPTED CONCLUSIONS
TRINITARIAN CONTROVERSY	Arius Eusebius of Nicomedia	Athanasius Hosius Basil the Great Gregory of Nyssa Gregory of Nazianzus Augustine of Hippo	Nicea (325) Constantinople (381)	Nicene Creed – Christ is "of the same substance with the Father." Father, Son, and Spirit are "coeternal, consubstantial, and coequal."
CHRISTOLOGICAL CONTROVERSY	Apollinarius Nestorius Eutyches	Cyril of Alexandria Theodoret Leo I	Constantinople (381) Ephesus (431) Ephesus ("Robber Synod") (449) Chalcedon (451)	Chalcedonian Definition – Christ is "one person in two natures, unmixed, unchanged, undivided, inseparable." Mary is "the Mother of God."
DONATIST CONTROVERSY	Donatus	Caecilian Augustine of Hippo	Arles (314)	"Outside the church there is no salvation."
PELAGIAN CONTROVERSY	Pelagius Coelestius John Cassian Caesarius of Arles	Augustine of Hippo Jerome	Ephesus (431) Orange (529)	Semi-Augustinianism; sacramental grace enables people to overcome their innate sinfulness.

Chart 24

Ancient Church Trinitarian Heresies

HERESY	MAJOR PROPONENTS	SUMMARY
MONARCHIANISM (Adoptionism)	Theodotus of Byzantium Paul of Samosata	Jesus became Christ at his baptism, was adopted by the Father after his death.
SABELLIANISM (Modalism, Patripassionism)	Sabellius Praxeus	One God reveals himself in three ways, or modes, at different times.
ARIANISM	Arius Eusebius of Nicomedia Eudoxius Eunomius	Christ is the first created being.
SEMI-ARIANISM (Eusebianism)	Basil of Ancyra Gregory of Laodicea	Christ is "of similar essence" with the Father, but is subordinate to him.
MACEDONIANISM (Pneumatomachism)	Macedonius	The Holy Spirit is a created being.

Chart 25

Ancient Church Christological Heresies

HERESY	MAJOR PROPONENTS	SUMMARY
APOLLINARIANISM	Apollinarius	Christ had no human spirit; the Logos replaced it.
NESTORIANISM	Nestorius	The Logos indwelt the person of Jesus, making Christ a God-bearing man rather than the God-Man. Affirmed merely mechanical rather than organic union of the person of Christ.
EUTYCHIANISM	Eutyches	The human nature of Christ was absorbed by the Logos.
MONOPHYSITISM	Severus Julian of Halicarnassus Stephanus Niobes	Christ had one nature (unwilling to accept impersonal human nature of Christ).
MONOTHELITISM	Theodore of Arabia Sergius Cyrus of Alexandria	Christ had no human will, just the one divine will.

Chart 26

The Pelagian Controversy

POSITION	MAJOR PROPONENTS	SUMMARY
PELAGIANISM	Pelagius Julian of Eclanum Coelestius	Man is born essentially good and capable of doing what is necessary for salvation. He sins because he follows bad examples, but Christ came to set a good example.
AUGUSTINIANISM	Augustine of Hippo	Man is dead in sin; salvation is totally by the grace of God, which is given only to the elect.
SEMI-PELAGIANISM	John Cassian Vincent of Lerins	The grace of God and the will of man work together in salvation, in which man must take the initiative.
SEMI-AUGUSTINIANISM	Caesarius of Arles	The grace of God comes to all, enabling a person to choose and perform what is necessary for salvation.

Chart 27

The Ecumenical Councils of the Early Church

LOCATION	DATE	EMPEROR	KEY PARTICIPANTS	MAJOR OUTCOMES
NICEA	325	Constantine	Arius Alexander Eusebius of Nicomedia Eusebius of Caesarea Hosius Athanasius	Declared Son *homoousios* (coequal, consubstantial, and coeternal) with Father. Condemned Arius. Drafted original form of Nicene Creed.
CONSTANTINOPLE	381	Theodosius	Meletius Gregory of Nazianzus Gregory of Nyssa	Confirmed results of Council of Nicea. Produced revised Nicene Creed. Ended Trinitarian controversy. Affirmed deity of Holy Spirit. Condemned Apollinarianism.
EPHESUS	431	Theodosius II	Cyril Nestorius	Declared Nestorianism heretical. Accepted by implication Alexandrian Christology. Condemned Pelagius.
CHALCEDON	451	Marcian	Leo I Dioscurus Eutyches	Declared Christ's two natures "unmixed, unchanged, undivided, inseparable." Condemned Eutychianism.
CONSTANTINOPLE	553	Justinian	Eutychius	Condemned "Three Chapters" to gain support of Monophysites. Affirmed Cyrillian interpretation of Chalcedon.
CONSTANTINOPLE	680–681	Constantine IV		Rejected Monothelitism. Condemned Pope Honorius (d.638) as heretical.
NICEA	787	Constantine VI		Declared veneration of icons and statues legitimate.

Chart 28

Monasticism in the Ancient Church

NAME	DATES	LOCATION	TYPE OF MONK	CONTRIBUTIONS
ANTHONY OF THEBES	c.251–356	Egypt	Anchorite	Initiated anchoritic practice as first hermit monk. Influenced many to practice monasticism. Encouraged martyrs during persecution of church in 311. Biography written by Athanasius.
PACHOMIUS	c.290–c.346	Egypt	Coenobite	Initiated coenobite practice by founding first monasteries. By his death, led nine cloisters for men, two for women.
HILARION	c.291–371	Palestine	Anchorite	Influenced by Anthony. First to bring anchorite practice to Palestine.
BASIL THE GREAT	c.329–379	Cappadocia	Coenobite	Founded monastery in Pontus. Founded first Christian hospital for care of lepers. His monastic rule still used in Eastern Church.
MACARIUS	d.c.390	Egypt	Anchorite	Influenced by Anthony. Supervised group of hermits in Libyan desert.
MARTIN OF TOURS	c.335–c.400	Gaul	Coenobite	Missionary to Franks. First to bring monasticism to the West. Served as bishop of Tours while living monastic life. First monk to be canonized.
JEROME	c.345–420	Syria Rome Bethlehem	Coenobite	Lived as an anchorite in Syria early in life. Encouraged asceticism in Rome. Founded monastery in a cave in Bethlehem, where he lived for 35 years while translating Vulgate.
AUGUSTINE OF HIPPO	354–430	North Africa	Coenobite	Converted under Ambrose in Milan after dissolute youth. Founded monasteries in North Africa as bishop of Hippo. Rule of St. Augustine influenced later ascetics.
JOHN CASSIAN	c.360–c.435	Gaul	Coenobite	Educated in monastery in Bethlehem. Founded monastery of St. Victor near Marseilles. Wrote in support of Semi-Pelagianism.
PATRICK	c.389–c.461	Ireland	Coenobite	Born in Britain, taken as slave to Ireland, where he later returned as missionary, converted over 100,000 Irish. Founded monastery at Armagh. Irish monasteries provided many missionaries for conversion of barbarian tribes.
SIMEON STYLITES	c.390–459	Syria	Anchorite	First of the pillar monks. Lived on a 50-foot pillar for the last 36 years of his life. Influenced many other stylites.
CASSIO-DORUS	c.477–c.570	Rome	Coenobite	Wealthy nobleman who founded monastery on his own estate. Introduced practice of copying manuscripts to monastic life.
BENEDICT OF NURSIA	c.480–c.543	Monte Cassino	Coenobite	Began as a hermit in Subiaco. Founded monastery at Monte Cassino, which became first monastery of Benedictine Order. Wrote Benedictine Rule.

Chart 29

Women in the Ancient Church

NAME	DATES	LOCATION	CONTRIBUTIONS
CECILIA	d.c.177	Rome	About to be married to pagan nobleman, converted him on eve of marriage; both beheaded shortly after.
MAXIMILLA	d.179	Phrygia	Two noblewomen who left their husbands and gave away their wealth to accompany Montanus, prophesying about the establishment of the millennium at Pepuza.
PRISCILLA	2nd century		
PERPETUA	d.203	Carthage	Young Montanist noblewoman martyred in the arena after extensive tortures.
FELICITAS	d.203	Carthage	Servant of Perpetua; martyred with her mistress shortly after she gave birth to a child in prison.
HELENA	c.250–c.330	Bithynia	Mother of Constantine. Visited Palestine around 325, supposedly discovered tomb and cross of Christ; built Church of the Holy Sepulcher and Church of the Nativity. Advanced veneration of relics.
MARCELLA	325–410	Rome	Wealthy widow who gave away her goods and vowed celibacy. Jerome used her home for monastic activities. Died after torture by Goths during sack of Rome by Alaric.
MACRINA	c.327–380	Cappadocia	Sister of Basil the Great and Gregory of Nyssa. Founded monastic community for women at Annesi.
MONICA	c.331–387	Tagaste	Mother of Augustine of Hippo. Her prayers and example of piety influenced her son's eventual conversion.
BRIGID	c.455–523	Ireland	Founded first convent in Ireland. Helped spread Christianity on the island.

Chart 30

THE
MEDIEVAL CHURCH
(476–1517)

A Timeline of the Medieval Church (c.500–c. 1500)

	500 AD–600 AD	600 AD–700 AD	700 AD–800 AD	800 AD–900 AD	900 AD–1000 AD
PEOPLE	Cassiodorus (c.477–c.570) Boethius (c.480–524) Benedict of Nursia (c.480–c.543) Augustine of Canterbury (d.605) Isidore of Seville (c.560–636)	Willibrord (658–739) Bede (c.673–735) John of Damascus (c.675–749) Boniface (680–754)	Alcuin (d.c.804) Paschasius Radbertus (c.785–865) Ratramnus (d.868)	Gottschalk (c.805–869) John Scotus Erigena (c.810–c.877)	
RULERS	Justinian (ruled 527–565)		Leo III (718–741) Pepin the Short (752–768) Charlemagne (768–814)		Otto I (936–973)
POPES	Gregory I (590–604)			Nicholas I (858–867)	
EVENTS	Benedictine Order founded (529) Council of Orange (529) Second Council of Constantinople (553) Augustine of Canterbury arrives in England (597)	Muslim Conquest (633–732) Synod of Whitby (663) Third Council of Constantinople (681)	Iconoclastic Controversy (725–843) Battle of Tours (732) Donation of Pepin (752) Second Council of Nicea (787)	Charlemagne crowned Holy Roman Emperor (800) Donation of Constantine (c.800) Pseudo-Isidorean Decretals (c.850)	Cluny monastery founded (910)

Chart 31

	1000 AD–1100 AD	1100 AD–1200 AD	1200 AD–1300 AD	1300 AD–1400 AD	1400 AD–1500 AD
PEOPLE	Lanfranc (c.1005–1089) Anselm (c.1033–1109) Peter Abelard (c.1079–1142) Bernard of Clairvaux (1090–1153) Hildegard of Bingen (1098–1197)	Peter Waldo (d.c.1215) Dominic Guzman (1170–1221) Francis of Assisi (1182–1226)	Bonaventure (1221–1274) Thomas Aquinas (1224–1274) John Duns Scotus (c.1266–1308) William of Ockham (c.1280–c.1349)	John Wycliffe (c.1329–1384) John Huss (1373–1415) Thomas à Kempis (c.1380–1471)	Francisco Jimenes (c.1436–1517) Savonarola (1452–1498)
RULERS	Henry IV (1080–1106)	Frederick Barbarossa (1152–1190) Philip Augustus I (1180–1223) Richard I (1189–1199)	Frederick II (1212–1250) Louis IX (1226–1270) Philip IV (1285–1314)		Sigismund (1410–1438)
POPES	Leo IX (1049–1054) Gregory VII (1073–1085) Urban II (1088–1099)	Innocent III (1198–1216)	Boniface VIII (1294–1303)		Martin V (1417–1431) Alexander VI (1492–1503)
EVENTS	Great Schism (1054) Reform of College of Cardinals (1059) Crusades (1095–1291)	Concordat of Worms (1122)	Magna Carta (1215) Fourth Lateran Council (1215) Dominicans founded (1216) Franciscans founded (1223) Aquinas's *Summma Theologica* (1273)	*Unam Sanctum* (1302) "Babylonian Captivity" of the Papacy (1309–1378) Great Papal Schism (1378–1417)	Council of Pisa (1409) Council of Constance (1414–1418) Council of Basel/ Ferrara (1431–1449) Fall of Constantinople (1453) Gutenberg Bible (c.1460) Fall of Grenada (1492)

Chart 31

The Conversion of the Barbarian Tribes

TRIBE	DATE OF CONVERSION	KEY MISSIONARIES AND RULERS
GOTHS	c.340	Ulfilas (Arian)
	c.720	Boniface (Wynfrith) (Catholic)
PICTS	c.400	Ninian
IRISH	c.435	Patrick
FRANKS	c.496	Clovis
SCOTS	c.563	Columba
ANGLES AND SAXONS	c.600	Augustine of Canterbury Ethelbert
FRISIANS	c.690	Willibrord

Chart 32

Church and State in the Byzantine Empire (c.500–1453)

EMPEROR	DATES OF REIGN	IMPACT ON CHURCH
JUSTINIAN	527–565	Advanced caesaropapism. Sought triumph of Chalcedonian Orthodoxy over Arianism and Monophysitism. Empress Theodora supported Monophysites. Built Hagia Sophia in Constantinople. Condemned some teachings of Origen as heretical. Condemned "Three Chapters" (including Theodore of Mopsuestia) by royal decree in 544, favored Christology of Cyril of Alexandria. Called Fifth Ecumenical Council at Constantinople in 553. Persecuted pagans, Manichaeans, Montanists.
HERACLIUS	610–641	Affirmed Monothelitism in 638.
CONSTANS II	641–668	Issued edict forbidding discussion of number of natures or wills of Christ. Tortured and exiled Pope Martin I and Maximus the Confessor for ignoring edict.
CONSTANTINE IV	668–685	Called Sixth Ecumenical Council at Constantinople in 680. Condemned Monothelites, declared Pope Honorius heretical.
JUSTINIAN II	685–695	Called council at Constantinople that widened gap between Eastern and Western churches by allowing deacons and presbyters to marry and rejecting other Western church practices.
LEO III (the Isaurian)	717–741	Promulgated edict against the veneration of icons in 726, initiating Iconoclastic Controversy. Decreed removal or destruction of all icons in 730. During his reign, Pope Gregory III excommunicated the iconoclasts.
CONSTANTINE V	741–775	Called council to condemn icons, persecuted those who venerated them.
LEO IV	775–780	Permitted icons outside Constantinople.
CONSTANTINE VI	780–797	Mother Irene served as regent, favored icons, and convened Seventh Ecumenical Council at Nicea in 787. Affirmed veneration of icons but regulated their use.

Chart 33

Church and State in the Byzantine Empire (c.500–1453) (continued)

EMPEROR	DATES OF REIGN	IMPACT ON CHURCH
LEO V (the Armenian)	813–820	Again banned icons, but without the persecution characteristic of earlier iconoclasts.
THEOPHILUS II	829–842	Persecuted, imprisoned, and mutilated monks who supported icons.
MICHAEL III	842–867	Mother Theodora served as regent, restored icons in 843, ending Iconoclastic Controversy. First Sunday in Lent celebrated as Feast of Orthodoxy in honor of restoration of icons. Deposed Ignatius as Patriarch of Constantinople, replacing him with Photius; action was overruled by Pope Nicholas I, further alienating Eastern and Western churches. Sent Cyril and Methodius to labor as missionaries among Slavs.
CONSTANTINE IX	1042–1055	During his reign the Great Schism occurred when Patriarch of Constantinople Michael Cerularius excommunicated Pope Leo IX.
ALEXIUS I COMNENUS	1081–1118	Issued summons for help that led to the First Crusade.
ALEXIUS II ANGELUS	1203–1204	Begged for assistance from Crusaders after his father Isaac II Angelus was blinded and deposed, offering to submit to the pope's authority. Crusaders sacked Constantinople and established Latin Crusader Kingdom there; Eastern church refused to back Alexius' promise.
JOHN III	1222–1254	Sought peace with Western church; conducted failed negotiations with popes Gregory IX and Innocent IV.
MICHAEL VIII PALEOLOGUS	1259–1282	Put an end to Latin Crusader Kingdom of Constantinople in 1261. Sought reunion with Rome at Second Council of Lyons in 1274, but gained only temporary success.
JOHN V PALEOLOGUS	1341–1376	Submitted to the pope on visit to Rome in 1369, but Byzantines refused to agree.
JOHN VIII PALEOLOGUS	1425–1448	Sought unity with Rome at Council of Basel/Ferrara in 1439 to try to save Byzantine Empire from Turkish invasion; agreement again repudiated by majority of Orthodox.
CONSTANTINE XI PALEOLOGUS	1449–1453	During his reign Constantinople fell to the Turks and the Byzantine Empire came to an end.

Chart 33

Church and State in the West (754–1309)

PERIOD	DATES	KEY EVENTS	LEADING FIGURES	CHARACTERISTICS
Holy Roman Empire of Charlemagne	754–962	754 – Donation of Pepin Mid 8th century – Donation of Constantine (forged) 800 – Crowning of Charlemagne Mid 9th century – Pseudo-Isidorean Decretals (forged) 840 – Division of empire among Charlemagne's grandsons	Pepin the Short (c.714–768) Charlemagne (742–814) Nicholas I (c.800–868)	Creation of Papal States made pope temporal ruler. Crowning of Charlemagne set stage for power struggle between church and state. Feudal fragmentation of society occurred. In latter part of period, papacy was held by unworthy men under domination of Roman barons ("Pornocracy").
Holy Roman Empire of Otto I	962–1059	962 – Otto I crowned Holy Roman Emperor by the pope 1044–1046 – Papal schism 1054 – Schism of Eastern and Western churches	Otto I (912–973) Leo IX (1002–1054)	Period was characterized by constant German interference in Italian and papal affairs. Popes were generally weak, puppets of Italian or German overlords. Growth of Cluny reform developed strong leadership for church.
Increase of Papal Domination	1059–1216	1059 – Papal elections entrusted to College of Cardinals 1077 – Henry IV humbled at Canossa by Gregory VII 1095 – Crusades begin 1122 – Concordat of Worms brings compromise in lay investiture controversy 1215 – Magna Carta 1215 – Fourth Lateran Council	Hildebrand (Gregory VII) (c.1021–1085) Urban II (1042–1099) Henry IV (1050–1106) Innocent III (1161–1216)	Hildebrandine reform greatly enhanced power of papacy. Lay investiture controversy reached its peak. Excommunication and interdict became potent weapons in papal arsenal. Papal power reached its zenith as Innocent III claimed absolute spiritual and temporal authority.
Decline of Papal Domination	1216–1309	1291 – Fall of Acre, end of Crusades 1302 – Papal bull Unam Sanctum 1309 – Beginning of the so-called Babylonian Captivity; papacy moved to Avignon, France	Boniface VIII (c.1234–1303) Philip IV (the Fair) (1268–1314)	Popes continued to make grandiose claims of temporal power but were less and less able to back them up. By the end of the period, the papacy fell completely under French domination after Philip IV kidnaped Boniface VIII.

Chart 34

The Iconoclastic Controversy

THOSE WHO SUPPORTED ICONS		THOSE WHO OPPOSED ICONS	
MAJOR ARGUMENTS	**KEY FIGURES IN THE EAST**	**MAJOR ARGUMENTS**	**KEY FIGURES IN THE EAST**
It is appropriate to use art in the service of the church. Pictures aided an illiterate population. Emotional attachment of common people, especially women, to icons necessitated the continuation of the veneration of icons. Icons were said to have performed miracles. Incarnation of Christ justifies his representation in human form. Icons combated Docetism and Monophysitism by showing the humanity of Christ. Use of icons reduced power of the state over the church. Icons, being two-dimensional, are not "graven images." Veneration is not the same as worship. Images bring truth to the eye while the Word brings it to the ear. Veneration of icons gives honor to what the icons represent. Icons serve as windows into the spiritual world. Popes supported use of images in worship.	Germanus (634–734) John of Damascus (c.675–c.749) Irene (755–803) Theodore of Studium (759–826) Constantine VI (771–797) Theodora (d.856)	Icons represented a compromise with paganism. Icons violated the second commandment. Many church fathers opposed the veneration of images. Veneration of icons constituted idolatry. Kissing, bowing, and burning incense before images are idolatrous practices. Icons contributed to the veneration of saints, which is idolatry (though not all iconoclasts opposed the veneration of saints). Images place false limits on the incomprehensibility of the Godhead. The bread and wine of the Eucharist are the only permissible representations of Christ. Worship of icons was the reason for conquest of Christian lands by Muslims. Removal of icons would gain support of strict Montanists. Removal of icons would reduce the power of monasteries, which produced them, while enhancing the power of the emperor. Alcuin's *Caroline Books* threw support of Carolingian Empire behind iconoclasts.	Leo III (675–741) Constantine V (718–775) Leo V (775–820) John the Grammarian (late 8th – early 9th centuries) Theophilus (813–842)
KEY FIGURES IN THE WEST		**KEY FIGURES IN THE WEST**	
Gregory II (pope 715–731) Gregory III (pope 731–741) Adrian I (pope 772–795)		Alcuin of York (c.735–804) Charlemagne (c.742–814)	

Chart 35

Early Medieval Church Leaders

NAME	DATES	PLACES OF MINISTRY	REPRESENTATIVE WRITINGS	NOTABLE FACTS
BOETHIUS	c.480–524	Athens Italy	*Consolation of Philosophy* *Opuscula Sacra*	Served in the court of Arian Ostrogoth king Theodoric. Saw philosophy as able to lead man to God. Was executed when accused of treason.
GREGORY THE GREAT	540–604	Rome	*Magna Moralia* *Dialogues*	Was born into aristocratic family. Entered Benedictine monastery. Was first monk to become bishop of Rome. Asserted authority of bishop of Rome over entire Western church. Constructed popular theology that influenced medieval church. Stimulated missionary effort in England. Protected Rome against the Lombards.
ISIDORE	c.560–636	Seville	*Scripture Allegories* *The Catholic Faith Defended Against the Jews* *Etymologies* *Three Books of Sentences*	Was named archbishop of Seville (600). Headed Council of Toledo (633). Was alleged in Middle Ages to be compiler of Pseudo-Isidorean Decretals.
BEDE	c.673–735	Northumbria	*Ecclesiastical History of England* *Life of St. Cuthbert of Lindisfarne*	Lived in monasteries from age seven. Never traveled more than a few miles from his birthplace. Gained most knowledge solely from monastery library.

Chart 36

Early Medieval Church Leaders (continued)

NAME	DATES	PLACES OF MINISTRY	REPRESENTATIVE WRITINGS	NOTABLE FACTS
JOHN OF DAMASCUS	c.675–749	Damascus Palestine	*Orations* *Fount of Knowledge*	Was born to Christian parents. Served in the court of Islamic caliph. Supported veneration of icons. Later left caliph's service to enter monastery. Produced a theology normative for Eastern church.
ALCUIN	735–804	York Aachen Tours	*The Trinity* *Life of St. Willibrord*	Was born into aristocratic family. Was educated at Cathedral School of York. Later became master of Cathedral School. Summoned as tutor to Charlemagne's court. Opposed adoptionists. Revised Jerome's Vulgate.
PASCHASIUS RADBERTUS	c.785–865	Soissons Saxony	*The Body and Blood of the Lord* *The Birth by the Virgin*	Was orphaned as young child. Entered Benedictine monastery. Was a proponent of doctrine of transubstantiation. Was a friend of Louis the Pious. Opposed Gottschalk.
RATRAMNUS	d.868	Corbie	*On Predestination* *On the Body and Blood of the Lord*	Was a pupil of Radbertus Opposed transubstantiation. Supported Gottschalk's view of double predestination. Writings cited by some Protestant Reformers to support their views.
GOTTSCHALK	805–868	Rheims	*The Eclogue of Theodolus*	As a child, was sent to monastery by parents. As an adult, tried to leave monastery but was not permitted to do so. Defended Augustinian doctrine of predestination, for which he was condemned and imprisoned. Was treated brutally, died after 20 years in prison, was denied Christian burial.
JOHN SCOTUS ERIGENA	c.810–c.877	Ireland France	*On Predestination* *On the Division of Nature*	Was born in Ireland. Served in the court of Charles the Bald in France. Was a Neoplatonist with pantheistic tendencies. Participated in predestinarian and Eucharistic controversies.

Chart 36

The Primary Causes of the East-West Schism of 1054

CAUSE	EASTERN CHURCH	WESTERN CHURCH
POLITICAL RIVALRY	Byzantine Empire	Holy Roman Empire
CLAIMS OF PAPACY	Patriarch of Constantinople was considered second in primacy to bishop of Rome.	Bishop of Rome claimed supremacy over the entire church.
THEOLOGICAL DEVELOPMENT	Stagnated after Council of Chalcedon.	Continued to change and grow through controversies and expansion.
FILIOQUE CONTROVERSY	Declared that the Holy Spirit proceeds from the Father.	Declared that the Holy Spirit proceeds from the Father and the Son.
ICONOCLASTIC CONTROVERSY	Engaged in 120-year dispute over the use of icons in worship; finally concluded they could be used (statues prohibited).	Made constant attempts to interfere in what was purely an Eastern dispute (statues permitted).
DIFFERENCES IN LANGUAGE AND CULTURE	Greek/Oriental	Latin/Occidental
CLERICAL CELIBACY	Lower clergy were permitted to marry.	All clergy were required to be celibate.
OUTSIDE PRESSURES	Muslims constricted and put continual pressure on Eastern church.	Western barbarians were Christianized and assimilated by Western church.
MUTUAL EXCOMMUNICATIONS OF 1054	Michael Cerularius anathematized Pope Leo IX after having been excommunicated by him.	Leo IX excommunicated Patriarch Michael Cerularius of Constantinople.

Chart 37

The Crusades

CRUSADE	DATES	CHIEF MOTIVATORS	NOTABLE PARTICIPANTS	GOAL	RESULTS
FIRST CRUSADE	1095–1099	Urban II Peter the Hermit	Walter the Penniless Peter the Hermit Raymund of Toulouse Godfrey Tancred Robert of Normandy	Liberate Jerusalem from the Turks.	Peter the Hermit led a horde of peasants toward the Holy Land but most died or were slaughtered en route. Crusaders captured Nicea, Antioch, Edessa, Jerusalem; established feudal Crusader kingdoms.
SECOND CRUSADE	1147–1148	Bernard of Clairvaux Eugene III	Konrad III Louis VII	Retake Edessa from Turks.	Mistrust between Western Crusaders and Eastern guides led to decimation of Crusader army; attempt to take Damascus failed.
THIRD CRUSADE	1189–1192	Alexander III	Frederick Barbarossa Philip Augustus Richard I	Retake Jerusalem from Saladin and the Saracens.	Frederick drowned; Philip returned home; Richard captured Acre and Joppa, made treaty with Saladin, and was captured and imprisoned in Austria on the way home.
FOURTH CRUSADE	1200–1204	Innocent II	Thibaut of Champagne Louis of Blois Baldwin of Flanders Simon de Montfort Enrico Dandolo	Undermine Saracen power by invading Egypt.	Christian city of Zara was sacked to repay Venice for transportation; for this the Crusaders were excommunicated; they then sacked Constantinople.
CHIL-DREN'S CRUSADES	1212	Nicholas of Cologne Stephen of Cloyes		Supernatural conquest of Holy Land by "the pure in heart."	Most of the children were drowned at sea, sold into slavery, or slaughtered.
FIFTH CRUSADE	1219–1221	Honorius II	William of Holland John of Brienne	Undermine Saracen power by invading Egypt.	Crusaders succeeded in taking Damietta in Egypt, but soon lost it again.
SIXTH CRUSADE	1229		Frederick II	Regain Jerusalem.	Crusaders made treaty with Sultan, giving Frederick control of Jerusalem; Frederick was excommunicated for this.
SEVENTH CRUSADE	1248		Louis IX	Relief of Holy Land through invasion of Egypt.	Crusaders were defeated in Egypt.

Chart 38

The Muslim Conquest and the Crusades—A Comparison

AREA OF COMPARISON	MUSLIM CONQUEST	CRUSADES
DATES	633–732	1095–1291
INITIATION	Death of Muhammad	Council of Clermont
TERMINATION	Battle of Tours	Fall of Acre
MOTIVATION	They desired to spread the true faith among the infidels by means of Jihad, or Holy War.	They sought to defend pilgrims and the glory of God and to recapture the holy places of Christendom from the infidel Turks.
INDUCEMENTS OFFERED	Immediate entrance to Paradise promised to those who die in Jihad.	Plenary indulgence offered— forgiveness of sins past, present, and future; for those who died, immediate entrance into heaven; for all others, forgiveness of debts and freedom from taxation.
TREATMENT OF ENEMIES	Pagans were required to convert or die; Jews and Christians were allowed to keep their religions but were required to pay tribute and refrain from proselytizing or public religious display.	Conquered Muslims were indiscriminately put to the sword; inhabitants of Jewish ghettos were slaughtered.
RESULTS	Palestine, Syria, Asia Minor, Egypt, North Africa, Spain were subjugated; Greek learning was preserved through the "Dark Ages."	No permanent territorial gains were made; classical Greek and Roman cultures were rediscovered; there was increased enmity between Eastern and Western churches and among Christians, Jews, and Muslims.

Chart 39

The Theology of Scholasticism

NAME	DATES	PLACES OF MINISTRY	REPRESENTATIVE WORKS	VIEW OF RELATIONSHIP OF FAITH AND REASON	VIEW OF NATURE OF UNIVERSALS	NOTABLE FACTS
ANSELM	1033–1109	Italy France Canterbury	*Monologium* *Proslogium* *Cur Deus Homo*	"Faith precedes knowledge."	Realist – *universalia ante rem*	Was born in Italy. Entered monastery in France. Became archbishop of Canterbury (1093). Opposed lay investiture. Devised ontological argument for the existence of God. Promulgated substitutionary view of the atonement.
PETER ABELARD	1079–1142	France	*Sic et Non* *Christian Theology* *Story of Misfortunes*	"Nothing is to be believed until it is understood."	Moderate Realist (or Conceptualist) – *universalia in re*	In early years had disputes with most of his teachers. Became head of Cathedral School in Paris. Fathered child out of wedlock with Hélöise. Was castrated by order of her uncle. Retired to monastery. Was condemned as a heretic by instigation of Bernard of Clairvaux.
BERNARD OF CLAIRVAUX	c.1090–1153	France	*Degrees of Humility and Pride* *Loving God*	"God is known so far as he is loved."	Mystic – Not an issue	Was born of noble parents. Entered Cistercian monastery (1113). Founded monastery in Clairvaux. In preaching encouraged Second Crusade. Was vehement opponent of Abelard. Was noted hymn writer.
PETER LOMBARD	1095–c.1159	Italy Paris	*Four Books of Sentences*	Dilemmas of faith to be resolved by reason.	Moderate Realist	Was born in northern Italy. Studied under Abelard. Became bishop of Paris. His *Sentences* became first standard medieval systematic theology. Emphasized seven sacraments.
HUGH OF ST. VICTOR	c.1096–1141	Saxony Paris	*Summa Sentimentarum*	Faith is a certainty "above opinion and below science."	Mystic	Was born in Saxony. Entered school of St. Victor in Paris, where he later became master.

Chart 40

NAME	DATES	PLACES OF MINISTRY	REPRESENTATIVE WORKS	VIEW OF RELATIONSHIP OF FAITH AND REASON	VIEW OF NATURE OF UNIVERSALS	NOTABLE FACTS
ALBERTUS MAGNUS	c.1200–1280	Bavaria Padua Paris Cologne	System of Nature The Praise of Mary	"Theology is science in the truest sense."	Moderate Realist	Was born in Bavaria. Entered Dominican order. Taught Aquinas. Became bishop of Regensburg. Was renowned student of natural sciences. Was knowledgeable in Aristotelian philosophy. Advanced veneration of Mary.
JOHN BONAVEN-TURE	c.1217–1274	Italy	On the Poverty of Christ Life of St. Francis Breviloquium Journey to the Mind of God	True knowledge comes only from the contemplation of the divine mystery.	Mystic	Was born in Tuscany. Entered Franciscan order at age 17. Became head of Franciscans. Advanced veneration of Mary. Was noted hymn writer.
THOMAS AQUINAS	c.1225–1274	Italy Paris Cologne	Summa Theologica Summa Contra Gentiles Contra Errores Graecorum	Natural reason leads on to the "vestibule of faith."	Moderate Realist	Was born to noble family in Aquino. Entered monastery at Monte Cassino at age five. Entered Dominican order at age 19. Studied under Albertus Magnus. Taught at Paris, Cologne, and throughout Italy. Leaned heavily on writings of Aristotle and Augustine.
JOHN DUNS SCOTUS	c.1266–1308	Britain Paris Cologne	Opus Oxoniense Questiones Quodlibetales	Knowledge of God cannot come from reason but must be accepted on the basis of the authority of the church. "A thing may be at the same time true in philosophy and false in theology."	Moderate Realist	Was born in British Isles. Entered Franciscan order. Studied and taught at Oxford. Earned doctorate in Paris. Was opponent of Aquinas. Influenced doctrine of Immaculate Conception. Protestants later coined the word "dunce" in reference to him.
WILLIAM OF OCKHAM	c.1280–1349	England Paris Munich	Summa Logicae Dialogus Inter Magistrum et Discipulum	"Doctrines peculiar to revealed theology are not susceptible to proof by pure reason."	Nominalist – universalia post rem	Was born in Surrey. Entered Franciscan order. Studied under Duns Scotus. Taught in Paris. Was excommunicated for his views. Opposed papal infallibility. Denied civil authority of church.

Chart 40

Arguments for the Existence of God—The Five Ways of Thomas Aquinas

ARGUMENT	OBSERVATIONS	IMPLICATIONS	CONCLUSION
FROM MOTION	Motion cannot initiate itself but must be motivated by something already in motion.	An infinite chain of movers is impossible, for then there would be no first mover and therefore no motion at all. The chain must have a beginning.	The unmoved Prime Mover is what we call God.
FROM CAUSALITY	Certain events are caused by prior events, which are themselves caused, etc.	As above, the causal chain cannot be infinite.	The uncaused First Cause is what we call God.
FROM POSSIBILITY	Certain things are transitory, their existence derivative. Their existence is possible rather than necessary.	The chain of derivative existence cannot be infinite but must find its source in a self-existent necessary Being.	This self-existent necessary Being is what we call God.
FROM IMPERFECTION	We judge certain things to have a lesser degree of perfection than others.	Relative assessments require an absolute standard of perfection. According to Aristotle, that which is greatest in truth is greatest in Being.	This absolute standard, God, must exist.
FROM DESIGN	Inanimate things function together to accomplish an ordered purpose.	This cannot occur by chance but requires an intelligent Designer.	This Designer is what we call God.

Chart 41

Major Monastic Orders

CLASSIFI-CATION	ORDER	FOUNDER(S)	DATE	PLACE OF ORIGIN	SIGNIFICANT MEMBERS	NOTABLE FACTS
	BENEDICTINES	Benedict of Nursia	529	Monte Cassino, Italy	Bede Boniface	Became first monastic order. Order was based on Benedictine Rule.
	KNIGHTS OF ST. JOHN (Hospitallers)	Raymund de Puy	1113	Jerusalem		Sought to care for pilgrims and later to fight in Crusades. In 1530 became Knights of Malta. Suppressed in 1798 by Napoleon. Were reestablished in 1834.
MILITARY ORDERS	KNIGHTS TEMPLAR	Hugo de Payens Godfrey St. Omer	1119	Jerusalem		Sought to defend pilgrims by force. Became wealthy and powerful. Were suppressed in 1312.
	TEUTONIC KNIGHTS	German Pilgrims	1190	Acre		Maintained hospitals in Holy Land. Did missionary work in Germany. Were suppressed in 1523, but moved to and conquered East Prussia. Became ancestors of Junker landlords.
	CLUNIACS	William of Aquitaine	910	Cluny, France	Gregory VII Urban II	Resulted from reform in Benedictine order. Followed Benedictine Rule.
BENEDIC-TINES	CISTERCIANS	Robert Molesme	1098	Citeaux, France	Eugene III Benedict XII Bernard of Clairvaux	Followed Benedictine Rule. Trappists are a branch of this order. Were suppressed in 1790.
	AUGUSTIN-IANS				Thomas à Kempis Gerhard Groote Martin Luther Gregory of Rimini	Followed Rule of St. Augustine. Some were mendicants.
AUGUS-TINIANS	PREMON-STRANTS	Norbert	1119	Premontre, France		Followed Rule of St. Augustine.

Chart 42

Major Monastic Orders (continued)

CLASSIFI-CATION	ORDER	FOUNDER(S)	DATE	PLACE OF ORIGIN	SIGNIFICANT MEMBERS	NOTABLE FACTS
INDEPEN-DENT	CARTHUSIANS	Bruno	c.1082	Chartreuse, France	Hugh of Lincoln	Followed Rule of the Carthusian Order. Were very strict; practiced self-flagellation.
	CARMELITES	Berthold	1156	Mt. Carmel	Teresa of Àvila John of the Cross	Traced origins somewhat dubiously to Elijah. Later became mendicants. Sixteenth-century reform movement became Discalced (Barefoot) Carmelites.
MENDI-CANTS	DOMINICANS	Dominic Guzman	1216	Spain	Thomas Aquinas Albertus Magnus Meister Eckhart Johann Tauler Bartolomeo de Las Casas Girolamo Savonarola Tomas de Torquemada	Used Rule of St. Augustine. Used by popes to root out heresy. Conducted Inquisition.
	FRANCISCANS	Francis of Assisi	1223	Italy	Bonaventure Duns Scotus William of Ockham Roger Bacon Nicholas of Lyra	Their original rule was taken from Scripture. Took vow of absolute poverty. Produced Capuchins in 1525.
	SOCIETY OF JESUS (Jesuits)	Ignatius Loyola	1540	Rome	Francis Xavier Robert de Nobili Matteo Ricci	Their rule was taken from Loyola's Spiritual Exercises. Were active in missions and education. Sought to eradicate Protestant Reformation. Were committed to absolute authority of the pope. Were suppressed in 1773. Were restored in 1814.

Chart 42

Medieval Mysticism

NAME	DATES	LOCATION	CONTRIBUTIONS
BERNARD OF CLAIRVAUX	1090–1153	Clairvaux, France	Founded monastery at Clairvaux. Preached Second Crusade; disappointed by its failure. Noted opponent of Peter Abelard. Influential mystic and hymn writer.
HUGH OF ST. VICTOR	c.1096–1141	Paris, France	Studied at Monastery of St. Victor, later headed its school. Wrote of three stages of insight—*cogitatio, meditatio, contemplatio.*
HILDEGARD OF BINGEN	1098–1179	Bingen, Germany	Founded and led several convents, wrote voluminously. Visions denounced corruption in government and church. Twenty-six visions recorded in Scivias with papal approval. Friend of Bernard of Clairvaux.
JOACHIM OF FIORE	c.1135–1202	Calabria, Italy	Became Cistercian monk; later founded own order. Taught that the present Age of the Son would end in 1260, when the Age of the Spirit, the Millennium, would begin.
FRANCIS OF ASSISI	1182–1226	Assisi, Italy	Founder of the Order of Friars Minor (Franciscans). Sought to live a life of poverty and service to the poor. Preached to Sultan of Egypt in an effort to evangelize Muslims. Supposedly received stigmata in mystical experience late in life.
JOHN BONAVENTURE	c.1217–1274	Tuscany, Italy	Joined Franciscans, of which he eventually became head. Studied under Albertus Magnus, worked with Thomas Aquinas. Considered mystical illumination superior to human reason.
MEISTER ECKHART	c.1260–c.1327	Hochheim, Saxony	Dominican monk who preached to other monks and nuns, encouraging them to seek union with God through mystical experience. Mystical view of union with God close to pantheism.
RICHARD ROLLE	c.1295–1349	Yorkshire, England	Trained at Oxford, but became a hermit on an estate at Hampole. Wrote *The Fire of Love*, influenced Lollards.
JOHANN TAULER	c.1300–1361	Strassburg, Germany	Dominican disciple of Meister Eckhart. Preached against righteousness by good works or sacraments. Opposed corruption in the church; admired by Luther.

Chart 43

Medieval Mysticism (continued)

NAME	DATES	LOCATION	CONTRIBUTIONS
HEINRICH SUSO	c.1300–1366	Überlingen, Baden	Dominican disciple of Meister Eckhart. Wrote *Book of Eternal Wisdom*, dialogue between Christ and himself, along with spiritual autobiography.
BIRGITTA (or Bridget)	1303–1373	Sweden	Converted after she and her husband had eight children. Vision led her to found Brigittine Order of nuns. Tried to convince Pope Gregory XI to end the Babylonian Captivity.
GERHARD (GEERT) GROOTE	1340–1384	Deventer, Netherlands	Founder of the Brethren of the Common Life. Popular preacher, drew many to life of mystical communion and following the example of Christ.
JULIAN OF NORWICH	c.1342–c.1413	Norwich, England	Benedictine anchoress who lived in an isolated cell adjacent to a church. Received 16 visions in 1373, recorded as *Revelations of Divine Love*.
CATHERINE OF SIENA	1347–1380	Siena, Italy	Became Dominican nun at 18, ministered to victims of Black Death. Claimed that Christ appeared to her in a vision, put a wedding ring on her finger, and that she then received the stigmata. Convinced Gregory XI to end the Babylonian Captivity; supported Roman popes during the Great Schism. Wrote *The Dialogue*, a conversation between herself and God the Father dictated while in a trance.
MARGERY KEMPE	c.1373–1433	Norfolk, England	Took vow of chastity after having 14 children. Saw visions on pilgrimage to Holy Land, which she recorded in the first English autobiography, *The Book of Margery Kempe*. Her hysterical warnings almost caused her fellow pilgrims to throw her overboard.
THOMAS À KEMPIS	c.1380–1471	Kempen, Germany	Member of Brethren of the Common Life. Wrote devotional classic *The Imitation of Christ*.
JOAN OF ARC	1412–1431	Domremy, France	At age 13 began hearing voices she believed came from God. Led French troops to victory at Orleans during Hundred Years' War. Captured, condemned for witchcraft, burned at the stake at Rouen.
CATHERINE OF GENOA	1447–1510	Genoa, Italy	Guelf noblewoman named after Catherine of Siena. Joined Franciscan nuns, served the poor. Wrote mystical works including *Dialogues on the Soul and the Body*.

Chart 43

Women in the Middle Ages

NAME	DATES	LOCATION	CONTRIBUTIONS
CLOTILDE	c.475–c.545	Gaul	Queen of the Franks, instrumental in conversion of husband Clovis. Lived in a convent for 35 years after her husband's death.
THEODORA	c.500–c.548	Constantinople	Byzantine empress, wife of Justinian, whom she influenced greatly. Supported asceticism, favored Monophysitism.
HILDA	614–680	Northumbria	Noblewoman converted at age 13. Founded Whitby Abbey, over which she ruled for 22 years.
LIOBA	c.700–782	Germany	Brought by Boniface to head convent of Tauberkirschofsheim. Wrote devotional poetry; had nuns read Scripture to her as she slept.
IRENE	c.752–803	Constantinople	Wife of Byzantine Emperor Leo IV; became empress on his death. Called Second Council of Nicea in 787, which reinstated use of icons.
HROTSVIT	932–1002	Saxony	Canoness in Abbey of Gandersheim in Saxony. First Saxon poet and first Christian dramatist.
HÉLÖISE	c.1098–1164	Paris	Pupil and later mistress of Peter Abelard, bore his son. Entered convent after birth of son, later became Mother Superior.
ELINOR OF AQUITAINE	1122–1204	Aquitaine	Ruled Aquitaine, later married Louis VII of France and Henry II of England, gave birth to Richard I (the Lion-Hearted) and King John. Scandalized many by traveling on Second Crusade in 1147–1148.
CLARE	c.1194–1253	Assisi	Influenced by preaching of Francis of Assisi. Founded Poor Clares in 1215, an order for women similar to the Franciscans.
ELIZABETH OF HUNGARY	1207–1231	Thuringia	Married Count of Thuringia at age 14, widowed at age 20. Established hospital for the poor in Marburg.

Chart 44

Medieval Dissenters and Heretical Groups

GROUP	CHARACTERISTIC TEACHINGS	NOTABLE FACTS
PAULICIANS	Dualistic Docetic Emphasized epistles of Paul. Similar to teachings of Marcion. Rejected Old Testament and epistles of Peter. Rejected all external religious exercises. Extremely ascetic.	Began in 7th century. Were restricted to Eastern church. Were persecuted by Eastern church. Declined in 12th century.
BOGOMILS	Dualistic Ascetic Sabellian view of Trinity. Rejected sacraments.	Were outgrowth of Euchites. Became prominent in Eastern Europe.
CATHARI (Patarenes, Albigensians)	Dualistic Docetic Rejected sacraments (except Consolamentum). Extremely ascetic; opposed marriage. Similar to Manichaeans. Believed themselves the only true church. Divided into Perfect (only ones saved) and Believers. Believed in reincarnation. Rejected Purgatory, indulgences. Often practiced suicide by starvation. Pacifistic	Began early 11th century. Were outgrowth of Paulicians and Bogomils. Followers were burned at stake throughout Europe. Their greatest strength was in southern France. Were targets of Inquisition and several crusades. Consolamentum involved placing gospel of John on chest of initiate to incorporate him into ranks of the Perfect.

Chart 45

GROUP	CHARACTERISTIC TEACHINGS	NOTABLE FACTS
WALDENSIANS	Simple communal lifestyle. Preached Scripture in vernacular. Emphasized Sermon on the Mount. Encouraged lay preaching. Permitted women preachers. Denied Purgatory.	Were founded by Peter Waldo (d.c.1215). Began in southern France. Were also called Poor Men of Lyons. Were anathematized for preaching without church's consent. Were persecuted in northern Italy, Austria. Accepted Reformation in 1532.
LOLLARDS	Encouraged lay preachers. Denied transubstantiation. Encouraged use of Bible in English. Pacifistic Condemned pilgrimages, auricular confession, veneration of images. Denied Purgatory, priestly celibacy.	Were followers of John Wycliffe. Some were martyred, but many recanted when put on trial. Lollard leader Sir John Oldcastle was the original model for Shakespeare's Falstaff.
HUSSITES	Emphasized authority of Scripture over church. Demanded partaking of cup by laity. Denied transubstantiation, veneration of saints, indulgences, auricular confession. Read Scripture in vernacular.	Were followers of John Huss. Split into Taborite and Utraquist factions. Later became known as Unitas Fratrum or Bohemian Brethren. Five crusades were directed against them. Council of Basel made compromise settlement with Hussites. Were influenced by Waldensians. Are perpetuated today in form of Moravian church.

Chart 45

The Great Schism of the Papacy (1378–1417)

DATE	ROMAN POPES	AVIGNON POPES	CONCILIAR POPES
1375		GREGORY XI (1370–1378) Died in 1378, setting stage for Schism.	
1378			
1381	URBAN VI (1378–1389) Ended "Babylonian Captivity" but caused Schism by alienating French cardinals.	CLEMENT VII (1378–1394) After three years of warfare with supporters of Urban VI, moved to Avignon in 1381.	
1384			
1387			
1390	BONIFACE IX (1389–1404)		
1393			
1396		BENEDICT XIII (1394–1417) Deposed by Council of Pisa in 1409, but refused to step down; deposed by Council of Constance in 1417; returned to Spain, convinced to his dying day that he was the true pope.	
1399			
1402			
1405	INNOCENT VII (1404–1406)		
1408			
1411	GREGORY VII (1406–1415) Deposed by Council of Pisa in 1409, but refused to step down; deposed by Council of Constance in 1415.		ALEXANDER V (1409–1410) Appointed at Pisa.
1414			JOHN XXIII (1410–1415) Deposed by Council of Constance in 1415.
1417			
1420			MARTIN V (1417–1431) Named by Council of Constance to end Schism.
1423			

Chart 46

Medieval Ecumenical Councils

COUNCIL	DATE	KEY PARTICIPANTS	RESULTS
LATERAN I	1123	Callistus II	Confirmed Concordat of Worms. Forbade marriage of priests. Granted indulgences to Crusaders.
LATERAN II	1139	Innocent II	Anathematized followers of antipope Anacletus II. Condemned schismatic groups. Confirmed decisions of Lateran I.
LATERAN III	1179	Alexander III	Condemned Cathari. Required two-thirds vote of cardinals for papal elections.
LATERAN IV	1215	Innocent III	Established Inquisition. Confirmed election of Emperor Frederick II. Denounced Magna Carta. Defined doctrine of transubstantiation. Confirmed Franciscans. Condemned Cathari and Waldensians. Prepared for Fifth Crusade.
LYONS I	1245	Innocent IV	Deposed Emperor Frederick II. Mourned loss of Jerusalem to Saracens.
LYONS II	1274	Gregory X	Reaffirmed filioque clause. Prohibited new monastic orders. Attempted to reunite Eastern and Western churches. Decided that cardinals were to receive no salary during papal elections.
VIENNE	1311–1312	Clement V	Suppressed Knights Templar. Attempted to encourage new crusade, but failed. Condemned Beguines and Beghards.
PISA	1409	Peter D'Ailly Peter Philargi Guy de Maillesec	Not considered an official ecumenical council. Asserted conciliar authority over papacy. Deposed Gregory XII (Rome) and Benedict XIII (Avignon) and elected Alexander V. Lacked power to enforce its decisions; left church with three rival popes.
CONSTANCE	1414–1418	John XXIII Sigismund Peter D'Ailly John Gerson	Ended papal schism by deposing all three claimants and appointing Martin V. Tried and executed John Huss. Affirmed authority of councils over church and insisted they be called as often as necessary.
BASEL/FERRARA	1431–1449	Martin V Eugene IV Julian Cesarini Nicholas of Cusa	Affirmed authority of council after pope tried to disband it. Pope used disunity of council to reassert his authority. Reached compromise settlement with Hussites. Moved to Ferrara after arrival of Eastern delegation.

Chart 47

Forerunners of the Reformation

NAME	DATES	CHALLENGES TO THE CHURCH			PERSONAL DETAILS
		DOCTRINE	PRACTICE	AUTHORITY	
THOMAS BRADWARDINE	c.1290–1349	Emphasized grace of God in salvation.			Was an English theologian and mathematician. Was named archbishop of Canterbury (1349). Died of Black Plague.
GREGORY OF RIMINI	d.1358	Emphasized grace of God in salvation.			Was an Italian philosopher. Became an Augustinian monk.
JOHN WYCLIFFE	c.1329–1384	Denied transubstantiation.	Opposed church's accumulation of wealth, sale of indulgences.	Emphasized authority of Scripture.	Was professor at Oxford University. Lordship doctrine favored by English nobles. Was forced into retirement as a result of Peasants' Revolt (1381). Translated most of Vulgate into English. His body was exhumed and burned in 1428.
JOHN HUSS	c.1373–1415	Defined church by Christlike living rather than by sacraments.	Opposed sale of indulgences, veneration of images.	Emphasized authority of Scripture.	Was a Bohemian priest. Became professor at University of Prague. Was burned at stake by order of Council of Constance.
JOHN OF WESSEL	d.1481	Emphasized grace of God in salvation. Denied transubstantiation.	Opposed sale of indulgences, priestly celibacy.	Emphasized authority of Scripture.	Was a German theologian. Taught at University of Erfurt. Died in prison after being convicted of heresy and after recanting.
GIROLAMO SAVONAROLA	1452–1498		Preached against papal immorality.		Was an Italian Dominican monk. Instituted Bonfire of the Vanities. Was hanged and burned for heresy in Florence.
DESIDERIUS ERASMUS	c.1466–1536		Attacked inconsistency and hypocrisy in the church.		Was a Dutch humanist. Compiled Greek text of the New Testament used by Luther. Debated Luther by letter concerning free will. *In Praise of Folly* mercilessly satirized failings of the church.

Chart 48

THE
REFORMATION
(1517–1648)

A Timeline of the Reformation in Germany (1517–1648)

	1450 AD–1490 AD	1490 AD–1530 AD	1530 AD–1570 AD	1570 AD–1610 AD	1610 AD–1650 AD
PEOPLE	Frederick the Wise (1463–1525) Johann Tetzel (c.1465–1519) Jacopo Cajetan (1469–1534) Andreas von Carlstadt (c.1480–1541) Martin Luther (1483–1546) Balthasar Hübmaier (c.1485–1528) Caspar Schwenkfeld (1489–1561) Thomas Münzer (c.1490–1525)	Hans Denck (1495–1527) Philip Melanchthon (1497–1560) Nicholas Storch (d.1530) Sebastian Franck (c.1499–c.1542) Jacob Hutter (d.1536) Charles V (1500–1556) Matthias Flacius Illyricus (1520–1575) Martin Chemnitz (1522–1586)	Zacharius Ursinus (1534–1583) Caspar Olevianus (1536–1587) Johann Arndt (1555–1621)	Jacob Boehme (1575–1624) Johann Gerhard (1582–1637)	
EVENTS		Ninety-five Theses (1517) Luther excommunicated (1520) Diet of Worms (1521) Melanchthon's *Loci Communes* (1521) Luther translates Bible into German (1521–1534) Peasants' Revolt (1525) Luther marries Katherine von Bora (1525) Marburg Colloquy (1529) Augsburg Confession (1530)	Smalcald War (1546–1555) Peace of Augsburg (1555)	Formula of Concord (1577)	Defenestration of Prague (1618) Thirty Years' War (1618–1648) Peace of Westphalia (1648)

Chart 49

A Timeline of the Reformation in Switzerland (1519–1575)

	1475 AD–1500 AD	1500 AD–1525 AD	1525 AD–1550 AD	1550 AD–1575 AD
PEOPLE	Johann Oecolampadius (1482–1531) Ulrich Zwingli (1484–1531) Guillaume Farel (1489–1565) Martin Bucer (1491–1551) Georg Blaurock (c.1492–1529) Conrad Grebel (1498–1526) Felix Manz (1498–1527) Machael Sattler (d.1527)	Robert Estienne (1503–1559) Heinrich Bullinger (1504–1575) Pierre Olivétan (c.1506–1538) John Calvin (1509–1564) Pierre Viret (1511–1571) Theodore Beza (1519–1605)		
EVENTS		Zwingli arrives in Zurich (1519) Zurich breaks with Rome (1524) Anabaptist movement begins (1525)	Schleitheim Confession (1527) Marburg Colloquy (1529) Kappel Wars (1529–1531) First edition of Calvin's *Institutes of the Christian Religion* (1535) Calvin arrives in Geneva (1536) First Helvetic Confession (1536)	Servetus burned in Geneva (1553) Second Helvetic Cnfession (1566)

Chart 50

A Timeline of the Reformation in France (c.1510–1685)

		1510 AD–1545 AD	1545 AD–1580 AD	1580 AD–1615 AD	1615 AD–1650 AD	1650 AD–1685 AD
PEOPLE	**HUGUENOTS**	Jacques Lefevre d'Etaples (1455–1536) Guillaume Farel (1489–1565) John Calvin (1509–1564) Peter Ramus (1515–1572) Gaspard de Coligny (1519–1572) François d'Andelot (1521–1569) Louis, Prince de Condé (1530–1569)	Philippe Duplessis–Mornay (1549–1623) Henry of Navarre (1553–1610)	Moses Amyraut (1596–1664)	Pierre Jurieu (1637–1713)	
	CATHOLICS	Catherine de Medici (1519–1589)	Henry of Guise (1550–1588) Charles of Lorraine (1554–1611) Francis de Sales (1567–1622) Marie de Medici (1573–1642)	Vincent de Paul (1581–1660) Cornelius Jansen (1585–1638) Armand du Plessis, Cardinal Richelieu (1585–1642) René Descartes (1596–1650) Giulio Cardinal Mazarin (1602–1661)	Blaise Pascal (1623–1662) Jacques Bossuet (1627–1704) Madame Guyon (1648–1717)	
RULERS		Francis I (1515–1547)	Henry II (1547–1559) Francis II (1559–1560) Charles IX (1560–1574) Henry III (1574–1589)	Henry IV (1589–1610) Louis XIII (1610–1643)	Louis XIV (1643–1715)	
EVENTS		Lefevre translates Old Testament into French (1528)	Failed Calvin–Coligny mission to Brazil (1555) Gallican Confession (1559) Tumult of Amboise (1560) Colloquy of Poissy (1561) Huguenots massacred at Vassy (1562) Wars of Religion (1562–1593) St. Bartholomew's Day Massacre (1572)	Henry of Navarre turns Catholic to ascend throne as Henry IV (1593) Edict of Nantes (1598)	Thirty Years' War (1618–1648) Three "Huguenot Wars" (1621–1628) Fall of La Rochelle (1628) Peace of Alais deprives Huguenots of political privileges (1629) France joins Protestant side in Thirty Years' War (1630) The *Fronde* (1648)	Edict of Nantes revoked (1685)

Chart 51

A Timeline of the Reformation in England and Scotland (c.1530–1688)

	1490 AD–1510 AD	1510 AD–1530 AD	1530 AD–1550 AD	1550 AD–1570 AD	1570 AD–1590 AD
PEOPLE	Thomas Wolsey (c.1474–1530) Thomas More (1478–1535) Thomas Cromwell (c.1485–1540) Hugh Latimer (c.1485–1555) Miles Coverdale (1488–1568) Thomas Cranmer (1489–1556) William Tyndale (c.1494–1536) John Hooper (c.1495–1555) Nicholas Ridley (c.1500–1555) Reginald Pole (1500–1558) Patrick Hamilton (1503–1528) Matthew Parker (1504–1575)	George Wishart (c.1513–1546) John Knox (c.1514–1572) John Foxe (1516–1587)	Thomas Cartwright (1535–1603) Thomas Helwys (c.1550–c.1616)	Robert Browne (c.1553–1633) Henry Jacob (1563–1624) John Smyth (c.1565–1612)	John Donne (1573–1631) William Laud (1573–1645) John Robinson (c.1575–1625) James Ussher (1581–1656) Alexander Henderson (c.1583–1646) Edward Herbert, Lord Cherbury (1583–1648)
RULERS	Henry VIII (1509–1547)		[Mary Queen of Scots (1543–1567)] Edward VI (1547–1553)	Mary Tudor (1553–1558)	Elizabeth I (1558–1603) [James VI of Scotland (1567–1625)]
EVENTS		Henry VIII declared "Defender of the Faith" by the pope (1521)	Cranmer becomes archbishop of Canterbury (1533) Act of Supremacy (1534) Dissolution of monasteries (1536) Six Articles (1539) Book of Common Prayer (1549)	Forty-two Articles (1553) Pole becomes archbishop of Canterbury (1556) Knox begins to reform Scotland (1559) Parker becomes archbishop of Canterbury (1559) Thirty-nine Articles (1563)	Defeat of Spanish Armada (1588)

Chart 52

A Timeline of the Reformation in England and Scotland (c.1530–1688) continued

	1590 AD–1610 AD	1610 AD–1630 AD	1630 AD–1650 AD	1650 AD–1670 AD	1670 AD–1690 AD
PEOPLE	Samuel Rutherford (c.1600–1661) Thomas Goodwin (1600–1679) John Milton (1608–1674)	Richard Baxter (1615–1691) John Owen (1616–1683) George Fox (1624–1691) John Bunyan (1628–1688) John Flavel (c.1630–1691) John Howe (1630–1706)	Joseph Alleine (1634–1668) Richard Cameron (c.1648–1680)	Matthew Henry (1662–1714)	
RULERS		James I (1603–1625)	Charles I (1625–1649)	Oliver Cromwell (1649–1658) Charles II (1660–1685)	James II (1685–1688)
EVENTS		Millenary Petition (1603) Hampton Court Conference (1604) Gunpowder Plot (1605) Pilgrims flee to Holland (1608)	King James Bible (1611) *Book of Sports* (1618) Puritans found Massachusetts Bay Colony (1629)	Laud becomes archbishop of Canterbury (1633) National Covenant (1638) English Civil War (1642–1648) Solemn League and Covenant (1643) Westminster Assembly (1643–1649) Rutherford's *Lex Rex* (1644) Milton's *Areopagitica* (1644) Commonwealth and Protectorate (1643–1660)	Restoration (1660) Five Mile Act (1665) Pentland Rising (1666)	Test Act (1673) Bunyan's *Pilgrim's Progress* (1678) Glorious Revolution (1688)

Chart 52

A Timeline of the Reformation in the Netherlands (c.1530–1648)

	1500 AD–1530 AD	1530 AD–1560 AD	1560 AD–1590 AD	1590 AD–1620 AD	1620 AD–1650 AD
PEOPLE	Desiderius Erasmus (c.1466–1536) Menno Simons (1496–1561) Jan Matthys (d.1534) Melchior Hoffmann (c.1500–c.1543) Duke of Alva (1508–1582) Jan of Leyden (c.1509–1536)	Jan van Oldenbarneveldt (1547–1619) Jacob Arminius (1560–1609)	Francis Gomarus (1563–1641) Simon Episcopius (1583–1643) Hugo Grotius (1583–1645) Gisbert Voetius (1588–1676)	Johannes Cocceius (1603–1699)	
DUTCH STADHOLDERS		William the Silent (1533–1584)			William III of Orange (1650–1702)
SPANISH KINGS	Charles V (1500–1556)		Philip II (1527–1598)		
EVENTS		Münster seized by Anabaptists (1534–1535) Dutch Revolt (1559–1579)	"Council of Blood" (1567–1573) Union of Utrecht (1579) Defeat of Spanish Armada (1588)	Dutch gain independence from Spain (1609) Synod of Dordt (1618–1619)	Thirty Years' War (1618–1648)

Chart 53

A Timeline of the Catholic Reformation (c.1500–1648)

	1475 AD–1510 AD	1510 AD–1545 AD	1545 AD–1580 AD	1580 AD–1615 AD	1615 AD–1650 AD
PEOPLE	Francisco Jimenes (1436–1517) Jacopo Cajetan (1469–1534) Lorenzo Campeggio (c.1472–1539) Bartolomé de las Casas (1474–1566) Jacopo Sadoleto (1477–1547) Thomas More (1478–1535) Gasparo Contarini (1483–1542) Ignatius Loyola (1491–1556) Reginald Pole (1500–1558) Francis Xavier (1506–1552)	James Laynez (1512–1565) Teresa of Ávila (1515–1582) Philip Neri (1515–1595) Peter Canisius (1521–1597) Charles Borromeo (1538–1584) Caesar Baronius (1538–1607) John of the Cross (1542–1591) Robert Bellarmine (1542–1621)	Matteo Ricci (1552–1610) Francis de Sales (1567–1622) Robert de Nobili (1577–1656)	Vincent de Paul (1581–1660)	
POPES		Leo X (1513–1521) Adrian VI (1522–1523) Paul III (1534–1549)	Paul IV (1555–1559) Pius V (1566–1572)		
RULERS		Charles V (1519–1556)	Mary Tudor (1553–1558) Philip II of Spain (1556–1598)	Matthias (1612–1619)	Ferdinand II (1619–1637)
EVENTS	Moors driven from Spain (1492)	Oratory of Divine Love (1517–1527) Diet of Worms (1521) Society of Jesus founded (1534)	Council of Trent (1545–1563) Smalcald War (1546–1555) Dutch Revolt (1559–1579) French Civil War (1562–1593) St. Bartholomew's Day Massacre (1572)	Defeat of Spanish Armada (1588)	Thirty Years' War (1618–1648) Huguenot Wars (1621–1628) Peace of Westphalia (1648)

Chart 54

Four Major Reformers

	MARTIN LUTHER	ULRICH ZWINGLI	JOHN CALVIN	JOHN KNOX
DATES	1483–1546	1484–1531	1509–1564	c.1514–1572
BIRTHPLACE	Eisleben, Germany	Upper Toggenburg, Switzerland	Noyon, France	Haddington, Scotland
EDUCATION	Leipzig	Vienna, Basel	Paris, Orleans	St. Andrews
ENTERED PRIESTHOOD	1507	1506		1536
REPRESENTA-TIVE WRITINGS	Ninety-five Theses On the Papacy at Rome Address to the German Nobility The Babylonian Captivity of the Church The Bondage of the Will Larger Catechism Smaller Catechism Lectures on Romans Lectures on Galatians Table Talk	Concerning Freedom and Choice of Food Sixty-seven Conclusions	Institutes of the Christian Religion Commentaries on 49 books of Scripture	The First Blast of the Trumpet Against the Monstrous Regiment of Women History of the Reformation of Religion within the Realm of Scotland
NOTABLE FACTS	Was influenced by Brethren of the Common Life. In 1505 entered Augustinian monastery. In 1508 began teaching at University of Wittenberg. In 1517 posted Ninety-five Theses. In 1520 was excommunicated. In 1521 was called to Diet of Worms. From 1521–1534 translated Bible into German. In 1525 opposed Peasants' Revolt. In 1525 married Katherine von Bora.	Was influenced by Erasmus. Entered priesthood as a respectable career. Opposed sale of mercenaries by Swiss. In 1518 was called to Zurich. His reformation went far beyond that of Luther. Some followers broke away to form Anabaptists, whom he persecuted. Was killed in battle against Catholic cantons.	Turned to Protestantism while studying law in Paris. In 1533 was forced to flee Paris. In 1536 was persuaded by Farel to help in reforming Geneva. Was forced out of Geneva, settled in Strasbourg, where he married. In 1541 returned to Geneva, led Reformation there. Protestant refugees from all over Europe came to Geneva, took Calvin's ideas with them.	Was influenced by Thomas Gwilliam, George Wishart. Spent 1½ years as a galley slave. In 1549 went to England, preached against Catholicism. In 1553 went to Geneva, influenced by Calvin. In 1558 published The First Blast just as Elizabeth ascended the throne. In 1559 returned to Scotland, led Reformation there.

Chart 55

Other German Reformers

NAME	DATES	EDUCATION	NOTABLE FACTS
ANDREAS VON CARLSTADT	c.1480–1541	Erfurt, Cologne	Was colleague of Luther at Wittenberg. Defended Ninety-five Theses in debate against Johann Eck. Condemned with Luther in papal bull. Broke with Luther; influenced Swiss Anabaptists.
THOMAS MÜNZER	c.1490–1525	Leipzig	Was influenced by Luther early in life. Became leader of Radical Reformation. Was associated with Zwickau prophets. Led Peasants' Revolt, was executed as a result. Bitterly hated Luther for condemning Peasants' Revolt.
PHILIPP MELANCHTHON	1497–1560	Heidelberg, Tübingen	Was influenced by Erasmus. Became professor of Greek at Wittenberg at age 21. Systematized and defended Luther's theology. Wrote first Protestant systematic theology, *Loci Communes*. Became known for attempts at reconciliation with Reformed and Catholics.
MATTHIAS FLACIUS ILLYRICUS	1520–1575	Venice, Wittenberg	Studied under Luther and Melanchthon. Became professor of Hebrew at Wittenberg. Broke with Melanchthon, whom he saw as a compromiser. Vehemently criticized all with whom he disagreed.
MARTIN CHEMNITZ	1522–1586	Wittenberg	Studied under Melanchthon. Taught philosophy at Wittenberg. Set up church order in Brunswick. Helped draft Formula of Concord.
ZACHARIUS URSINUS	1534–1583	Wittenberg	Visited Calvin at Geneva. Taught at Breslau, Heidelberg. With Caspar Olevianus wrote Heidelberg Catechism. Became leader in German Reformed church.
CASPAR OLEVIANUS	1536–1587	Paris, Orleans, Bourges, Geneva	Was born in France. Studied under Calvin and Beza. Helped organize church in Heidelberg along Reformed lines. With Zacharias Ursinus wrote Heidelberg Catechism.

Chart 56

Other Swiss Reformers

NAME	DATES	EDUCATION	NOTABLE FACTS
JOHANN OECOLAMPADIUS	1482–1531	Bologna Heidelberg	Was trained in law, theology. Became a noted philologist. Was influenced by Erasmus, Melanchthon, Luther. Took the lead in bringing Reformation to Basel. Took part in Marburg Colloquy. Was a close associate of Zwingli.
GUILLAUME FAREL	1489–1565	Paris	Studied under Jacques Lefèvre. Was expelled from France, became traveling evangelist in Switzerland. Was influential in bringing Bern and Geneva into Reformation. Convinced Calvin to work on reforming church in Geneva. Spent latter part of life in Neuchatel.
MARTIN BUCER	1491–1551	Heidelberg	Was called the Peacemaker of the Reformation. Was a Dominican monk. Erasmus influenced him in direction of humanism. After hearing Luther, he became Lutheran, left Dominicans. Led Reformation in Strasbourg, where he influenced Calvin. Often attempted to reconcile warring Lutherans, Reformed, and Catholics. Taught at Cambridge by special invitation from Thomas Cranmer.
ROBERT ESTIENNE	1503–1559		Royal printer for Francis I of France (1539–1551). Arrived in Geneva in 1551. His Greek Bible became the basis for the Textus Receptus. His division of New Testament into verses was later used in the Geneva Bible.
HEINRICH BULLINGER	1504–1575	Cologne	Was influenced by Erasmus, Luther, Melanchthon. Succeeded Zwingli as religious leader of Zurich. Helped write First and Second Helvetic Confessions. Opposed presbyterianism.
PIERRE OLIVÉTAN	c.1506–1538	Paris Orleans	Cousin of Calvin who influenced him to adopt Protestantism. Fled to Strasbourg in 1528, Geneva in 1533. Translated Bible into French in Geneva.

Chart 57

Other Swiss Reformers (continued)

NAME	DATES	EDUCATION	NOTABLE FACTS
PIERRE VIRET	1511–1571	Paris	Studied under Lefèvre in Paris. Ordained by Farel in 1531. Helped prepare Geneva for reform under Calvin. Leading Reformer in Lausanne.
THEODORE BEZA	1519–1605	Orleans	Was trained in law. Turned to Protestantism in 1548 after severe illness. Taught Greek at Lausanne and Geneva. Headed Academy in Geneva. Defended Reformed Protestantism at Colloquy of Poissy in 1561. Succeeded Calvin as religious leader of Geneva. Discovered Codex Bezae. Was advisor to French Huguenots.

Chart 57

The Radical Reformation

CLASSIFICATION		KEY LEADERS	AREAS OF ACTIVITY	DISTINCTIVES	COMMON EMPHASES
ANABAPTISTS	PRIMITIVISTS	Andreas von Carlstadt Conrad Grebel Felix Manz Georg Blaurock Michael Sattler	Zurich and elsewhere in Switzerland	Sought return to New Testament church. Persecuted by Zwingli and others. Sattler produced Schleitheim Confession.	Repudiated church-state ties. Church considered voluntary association of committed believers. Repudiated infant baptism. Advocated religious toleration. Emphasized Scripture, Apostles' Creed. Questioned doctrinal conclusions and ecumenical councils of the Ancient Church.
		Jacob Hutter Balthasar Hübmaier	Moravia, later Dakotas and Western Canada	Community of property. Known for fine craftsmanship.	
	REVOLUTIONARIES	Thomas Münzer Nicholas Storch	Wittenberg, Zwickau, and elsewhere in Germany	Sparked Peasants' Revolt (1525).	
		Melchior Hoffmann Jan Matthys Jan of Leyden	Netherlands; especially Münster	Set up Old Testament theocracy in Münster in anticipation of Second Coming.	
	PACIFISTS	Menno Simons	Netherlands, later Russia, Pennsylvania, and elsewhere	Pacifists Simple lifestyle. Strict church discipline. Followers became Mennonites and Amish.	
		Jacob Ammann	Switzerland, later Pennsylvania and elsewhere		
SPIRITUALISTS		Hans Denck Sebastian Franck Caspar Schwenkfeld	Germany, later Pennsylvania	Mystics	
RATIONALISTS		Michael Servetus	France, Geneva	Anti-trinitarians Advocated soul sleep, annihilation of wicked.	
		Laelius Socinus Faustus Socinus	Italy, Poland, later England		

Chart 58

Italian Renaissance Figures and Their Relationship to the Church

NAME	DATES	ACHIEVEMENTS	RELATIONSHIP TO CHURCH
FRA ANGELICO	1378–1455	Florentine painter Works include *The Coronation of the Virgin*, *The Last Judgment*.	Dominican monk Believed one must be Christlike to paint Christ. Commissioned by Nicholas V to paint chapel in the Vatican.
LORENZO VALLA	c.1406–1457	Roman humanist, classical scholar, and linguist Proved Donation of Constantine a forgery in 1440.	Served as secretary to Pope Nicholas V despite his debunking of the famous document used to justify papal power.
FRA LIPPO LIPPI	c.1406–1469	Florentine painter Works include frescoes on *The Life of St. John the Baptist* and *Life of St. Stephen* in Prato Cathedral.	Was Carmelite monk 1421–1432. Became prior of Prato Cathedral.
MARSILIO FICINO	1433–1499	Florentine humanist Taught at Platonic Academy, wrote *Theologia Platonia*, *Of the Christian Religion*.	Catholic priest Believed classics of Greek thought could be related to biblical teaching.
SANDRO BOTTICELLI	1444–1510	Florentine painter Works include *Primavera*, *The Birth of Venus*, *The Adoration of the Magi*.	Turned to religious subjects by preaching of Savonarola. Painted scenes from life of Moses in Sistine Chapel.
LORENZO DE MEDICI	1449–1492	Duke of Florence and patron of the arts Oversaw Golden Age of Florentine art.	Rebuked by Savonarola, but respected him enough to call for him on his deathbed. Father of Pope Leo X and Catherine de Medici.
LEONARDO DA VINCI	1452–1519	Florentine painter, sculptor, architect, engineer, and scientist—the quintessential Renaissance Man. Paintings include *Mona Lisa*. Served in courts of Cesare Borgia, Louis XII, and Francis I.	Among his greatest religious paintings are *The Virgin of the Rocks* and *The Last Supper*.
PICO DELLA MIRANDOLA	1463–1494	Florentine humanist and philosopher In 1486, at age 23, offered to debate all comers on 900 theses covering all of human knowledge.	Tried to connect Greek philosophy and biblical truth. Believed Jewish Kabbala contained the key to Christian mysteries. Influenced late in life by Savonarola.
FRA BARTOLOMMEO	1475–1517	Florentine painter Painted *Head of St. Peter* with Raphael.	Follower of Savonarola, painted portraits of Florentine Reformer. Destroyed his nudes in Bonfire of the Vanities. Became Dominican monk in 1500.
MICHELANGELO BUONARROTI	1475–1564	Tuscan painter, sculptor, architect, and poet Paintings include *The Last Judgment*; sculptures include *David* and a *Pieta*.	Commissioned by Julius II to paint ceiling of Sistine Chapel. Designed dome of St. Peter's in Rome.
RAPHAEL	1483–1520	Renaissance painter and architect Paintings include the *Sistine Madonna* and *The Transfiguration*.	Court painter in the Vatican under Leo X Succeeded Bramante as chief architect of St. Peter's in Rome.

Chart 59

Northern Renaissance Figures and Their Relationship to the Church

NAME	DATES	COUNTRY	ACHIEVEMENTS	RELATIONSHIP TO CHURCH
JOHANN GUTENBERG	1398–1468	Germany	Invented moveable-type printing.	First printed book was the Bible. Later printed other religious books.
NICHOLAS OF CUSA	c.1401–1464	Germany	German philosopher, astronomer, mathematician, and mystic Affirmed rotation of earth's axis before Copernicus.	Educated by Brethren of the Common Life. Questioned Donation of Constantine, sale of indulgences. Supported Conciliar Movement in challenging papal authority; later submitted and became a cardinal.
JACQUES LEFÈVRE D'ÉTAPLES	c.1455–1536	France	French humanist, studied the works of Aristotle. Sought to devise a system of theology based on Scripture alone.	Translated Bible into French. Influenced Farel and Calvin.
DESIDERIUS ERASMUS	c.1466–1536	Netherlands	Dutch humanist and writer Works include *In Praise of Folly, Handbook of the Christian Knight*, and *The Freedom of the Will*.	Educated by Brethren of the Common Life. Became Augustinian monk. Opposed Luther's teaching on the bondage of the human will. Prepared Greek text of New Testament that became the basis for Protestant translations into vernacular.
ALBRECHT DÜRER	1471–1528	Germany	Best known for his woodcuts, including *Praying Hands* and *The Four Horsemen of the Apocalypse*. Paintings include *Four Apostles*. Court painter for Emperor Charles V	Never left Catholic Church, but was sympathetic to the Reformation. Friend of Luther, Melanchthon, and Erasmus.
LUCAS CRANACH (the Elder)	1472–1553	Germany	German painter and woodcut artist Court painter of Saxony Painted *Crucifixion*, but also many nudes.	Friend of Luther and Melanchthon, whose portraits he painted.
THOMAS MORE	1478–1535	England	English humanist and writer and friend of Erasmus, best known for *Utopia*. Served as Lord Chancellor under Henry VIII.	Probably ghost-wrote Henry VIII's *Defense of the Seven Sacraments*. Beheaded for refusing Oath of Supremacy.
HANS HOLBEIN (the Younger)	c.1497–1543	Germany	German painter and portraitist Altarpieces in Basel and Freiburg, along with many portraits. *Noli me tangere* for Hampton Court palace.	Befriended and encouraged by Erasmus and More, whose portraits he painted, along with those of Henry VIII and his wives Jane Seymour and Anne of Cleves.

Chart 60

The English Reformers

NAME	DATES	EDUCATION	NOTABLE FACTS
WILLIAM TYNDALE	c.1494–1536	Oxford Cambridge	Was forced into exile, published translation of New Testament in English while in hiding on the Continent. Was hounded all over Europe by his enemies. Was arrested and burned at the stake in Brussels.
THOMAS CROMWELL	c.1485–1540	Unknown	Was assistant to Cardinal Wolsey. Became a member of Parliament. Held office of vicar-general under Henry VIII. Supervised dissolution of monasteries. Encouraged translation and publication of Great Bible. Attempted to arrange a marriage alliance between Henry VIII and German Lutherans (Anne of Cleves). Was beheaded for treason.
HUGH LATIMER	c.1485–1555	Cambridge	In 1535 became bishop of Worcester. Was twice imprisoned by Henry VIII. Became leading preacher during reign of Edward VI. Was burned at the stake at Oxford under Mary Tudor.
NICHOLAS RIDLEY	c.1500–1555	Cambridge	Was chaplain to Cranmer, later to Henry VIII. In 1547 was named bishop of Rochester. In 1550 was named bishop of London. Helped produce first and second Book of Common Prayer. Was arrested and burned at stake with Latimer.
JOHN HOOPER	c.1495–1555	Oxford	Entered Augustinian monastery. Was converted to Protestantism, forced to flee country. Became friend of Bullinger while in Zurich. Became bishop of Gloucester and Worcester. Was burned at stake under Mary Tudor.
THOMAS CRANMER	1489–1556	Cambridge	Supported Henry VIII in effort to divorce Catherine of Aragon. In 1533 was named archbishop of Canterbury. Introduced moderate reforms under Henry VIII and Edward VI. Invited Martin Bucer to teach at Cambridge. Worked on production of first and second Book of Common Prayer. Was arrested and convicted of treason and heresy under Mary Tudor. Recanted under duress; burned at stake while repudiating his recantation.
MILES COVERDALE	1488–1568	Cambridge	Entered Augustinian monastery. Left monastery when converted to Protestantism; was forced to flee country. Assisted Tyndale in his translation work. Completed Tyndale's translation after Tyndale's death. Worked on Great Bible and Geneva Bible. In 1551 was named bishop of Exeter. Was exiled under Mary Tudor.
MATTHEW PARKER	1504–1575	Cambridge	Was chaplain to Anne Boleyn. Was a friend of Bucer when latter was in England. Was forced into hiding under Mary Tudor. In 1559 reluctantly accepted appointment as archbishop of Canterbury. Worked on Elizabethan Settlement. Opposed Puritans.

Chart 61

Church and State in Tudor England

MONARCH AND DATES	YEARS OF REIGN	RELIGIOUS ORIENTATION	NOTABLE FACTS AND EVENTS
HENRY VIII (1491–1547)	1509–1547	Roman Catholic	1509 – Married Catherine of Aragon, his brother Arthur's widow, by special papal dispensation. 1521 – Wrote *In Defense of the Seven Sacraments* against Luther; given title Defender of the Faith by the pope. 1528 – Obsessed with desire for male heir, he sought papal dispensation to divorce Catherine; request refused. 1533 – Repudiated papal authority, appointed Thomas Cranmer as archbishop of Canterbury, divorced Catherine, married Anne Boleyn. 1534 – Declared Supreme Head of the Church in England; dissolved monasteries. 1535 – Executed Thomas More for opposing Supremacy. 1539 – Promulgated Six Articles, affirming Catholic doctrine. 1540 – Attempt to ally with German Protestants failed with marriage to Anne of Cleves and subsequent divorce.
EDWARD VI (1537–1553)	1547–1553	Protestant	Son of Henry VIII and Jane Seymour Precocious but sickly king, he left rule of kingdom to regents but encouraged growth of Protestantism. Cranmer, Latimer, and Ridley flourished during his reign. Attempted through his will to prevent the succession of a Catholic ruler by leaving the throne to Lady Jane Grey, but failed. 1547 – Repealed Six Articles. 1549 – First Book of Common Prayer 1552 – Second Book of Common Prayer 1553 – Forty-two Articles
MARY (1516–1558)	1553–1558	Roman Catholic	Daughter of Henry VIII and Catherine of Aragon Declared illegitimate when her father divorced her mother. 1553 – Brought Cardinal Pole to England as her advisor. 1554 – Married Philip II of Spain against popular sentiment. 1555 – Initiated persecutions that gave her the name "Bloody Mary," costing the lives of over 300 Protestants, including Latimer, Ridley, Hooper, and Cranmer.
ELIZABETH I (1533–1603)	1558–1603	Protestant	Daughter of Henry VIII and Anne Boleyn Declared illegitimate after her mother was beheaded. Feigned Catholicism during Mary's reign. Charted moderate Protestant course during reign, alienating only obdurate Catholics and convinced Puritans. 1561 – Severed ties with the pope. 1570 – Excommunicated by the pope. 1571 – Thirty-nine Articles 1587 – Executed cousin Mary Stuart (Mary Queen of Scots). 1588 – Defeat of Spanish Armada 1603 – Dying without an heir, she named James VI of Scotland, son of Mary Stuart, as her successor.

Chart 62

The English Puritans

NAME	DATES	EDUCATION	ECCLESIASTICAL AFFILIATION	REPRESENTATIVE WRITINGS	NOTABLE FACTS
THOMAS CART-WRIGHT	1535–1603	Cambridge	Presbyterian	*Holy Discipline*	Lost teaching post at Cambridge for advocating presbyterianism. Spent time in Geneva. Was imprisoned several times for defense of Puritanism.
HENRY JACOB	1563–1624	Oxford	Congregational		Was part of Brownist movement. Became a member of John Robinson's church in Leyden. Founded first permanent Congregational church in England at Southwark.
OLIVER CROMWELL	1599–1658	Cambridge	Congregational		Was a member of Parliament from 1628. Led Parliamentary army during Civil War. Became Lord Protector of England after execution of Charles I. Refused proffered crown in 1656.
THOMAS GOODWIN	1600–1679	Cambridge	Congregational	Sermon collections	Became a Separatist through influence of John Cotton. Moved to the Netherlands after harassment by Archbishop Laud. Led Congregationalists at Westminster Assembly. Became an advisor to Cromwell.
JOHN MILTON	1608–1674	Cambridge	Congregational	*Areopagitica* *Paradise Lost*	Was a Puritan poet and pamphleteer. Decided against Anglican ministry because of Archbishop Laud. Was in government service under Cromwell. Was forced into retirement by Restoration. Held unorthodox views, including Arianism.

Chart 63

NAME	DATES	EDUCATION	ECCLESIASTICAL AFFILIATION	REPRESENTATIVE WRITINGS	NOTABLE FACTS
RICHARD BAXTER	1615–1691		Anglican	*The Saints' Everlasting Rest* *The Reformed Pastor* *A Call to the Unconverted*	Took mediating position in political and theological disputes of his day. Briefly served as chaplain to Charles II.
JOHN OWEN	1616–1683	Oxford	Congregational	*The Epistle to the Hebrews* *The Death of Death in the Death of Christ*	Entered Oxford at age 12; received master's degree at age 19. Supported Parliamentary cause in Civil War. Served as chaplain to Cromwell. Became vice-chancellor at Oxford.
JOHN BUNYAN	1628–1688		Baptist	*Pilgrim's Progress* *The Holy War* *Grace Abounding to the Chief of Sinners*	Was a tinker by trade. Fought in Parliamentary army. Became a Baptist preacher in Bedford. Was imprisoned for 12 years after Restoration.
JOHN FLAVEL	c.1630–1691	Oxford	Presbyterian	*Treatise on the Soul* *The Methods of Grace*	Was a pastor at Dartmouth until forced out by Clarendon Code. Returned to pastorate in 1671.
JOHN HOWE	1630–1706	Cambridge Oxford	Anglican	*Blessedness of the Righteous*	For many years was pastor at Great Torrington. Became a chaplain to Oliver and later Richard Cromwell. Was among more irenic of the Puritans.
JOSEPH ALLEINE	1634–1668	Oxford	Presbyterian	*An Alarm to the Unconverted*	Was imprisoned in 1663 for singing psalms and preaching to his family in his own home.
MATTHEW HENRY	1662–1714	By father at home	Presbyterian	*Matthew Henry's Commentary*	Originally studied law. Served as pastor at Chester, 1687–1712. Wrote six-volume devotional commentary still widely used.

Chart 63

Church and State in Stuart England

MONARCH AND DATES	YEARS OF REIGN	RELIGIOUS ORIENTATION	NOTABLE FACTS AND EVENTS
JAMES I (1566–1625)	1603–1625	Anglican	Son of Mary Queen of Scots and Lord Darnley Became James VI of Scotland at age 1 when his mother abdicated. Raised by Scottish nobles, but belief in Divine Right of Kings led him to oppose presbyterianism. Settled Protestant English and Scots in Ulster. 1587 – Attempted to impose episcopacy on Scotland. 1603 – Received Millenary Petition from English Puritans. 1604 – Rejected Puritan demands at Hampton Court Conference. 1605 – Gunpowder Plot assassination attempt by Catholics. 1611 – Publication of Authorized Version of the Bible 1618 – *Book of Sports* encourages exercise on Sundays.
CHARLES I (1600–1649)	1625–1648	High Church Anglican	Son of James I and Anne of Denmark 1625 – Married Henrietta Maria, daughter of Henry IV of France. 1627 – Sent military support to Huguenots at La Rochelle. 1629–1640 – Ruled without help of Parliament. 1633 – Appointed William Laud as archbishop of Canterbury, who then persecuted Puritans. 1637 – Attempted to impose episcopacy on Scotland, leading to signing of National Covenant. 1640 – Revolt in Scotland led to convening of Puritan-dominated Long Parliament. 1642–1648 – Civil war between Royalist and Parliamentary forces 1643 – Parliament accepts Solemn League and Covenant. 1643–1648 – Westminster Assembly 1649 – Beheaded for treason after calling for Scottish invasion.
COMMONWEALTH AND PROTECTORATE UNDER OLIVER CROMWELL	1648–1660	Puritan	Oliver Cromwell led Parliamentary forces during Civil War. 1648–1652 – Commonwealth under Parliamentary rule 1652 – Parliament disbanded 1653 – Cromwell named Lord Protector, ruling as military dictator until his death. Refused kingship when offered. Favored Congregationalism, opposed bishops and presbyters. Attempted to improve morals of the country by banning immoral entertainments, including closing theaters. 1658 – Oliver Cromwell dies, succeeded by son Richard. 1659 – Parliament invites Charles II to return from exile in France.
CHARLES II (1630–1685)	1660–1685	Covertly Catholic	Son of Charles I and Henrietta Maria Passed laws against Puritans and Covenanters, including Clarendon Code. 1670 – Signed secret Treaty of Dover with Louis XIV of France to bring England back to Catholicism. 1673 – By Test Act, Parliament excludes Catholics from public office. 1685 – Professed Catholicism on his deathbed.
JAMES II (1633–1701)	1685–1688	Overtly Catholic	Brother of Charles II; openly professed Catholicism. Ignored Test Act, promoting Catholics to high office. 1688 – Birth of son who was baptized Catholic led to Glorious Revolution when Parliament invited William of Orange to assume the throne.
WILLIAM III (1650–1702)	1688–1702	Tolerant Calvinist	Married Mary, oldest daughter of James II. Assumed throne of England in Glorious Revolution of 1688. Chief opponent of Louis XIV's expansionist ambitions 1689 – Bill of Rights 1690 – Defeated Catholic uprising in Ireland at Battle of the Boyne.
ANNE (1665–1714)	1702–1714	High Church Anglican	Daughter of James II; did not share Catholicism of her parents. Favored High Church, disliked Dissenters and Latitudinarians.

Chart 64

Leaders of the French Huguenots

NAME	DATES	ROLE IN MOVEMENT	NOTABLE FACTS
GASPARD DE COLIGNY	1519–1572	Military Leader	Was born into noble family. Became admiral of France in 1552. Became Protestant while in Spanish prison in the Netherlands. Was advisor to Charles IX. Established Huguenot colonies in Brazil and Florida. Was murdered in St. Bartholomew's Day massacre.
ANNE DU BOURG	c.1520–1559	Martyr	Was trained in law. Taught at University of Orleans. Became outspoken advocate of Protestantism in 1559. Was condemned for heresy, strangled, and burned.
PHILIPPE DUPLESSIS-MORNAY	1549–1623	Statesman	Was advisor to Henry of Navarre. Was appointed ambassador to England and the Netherlands. Served as governor of Saumur. Founded University of Saumur. Wrote in defense of the Reformed faith.
HENRY IV	1553–1610	Military Leader	Was born into Huguenot Bourbon family of Navarre. Married Catholic Margaret of Valois in 1572. Led Huguenots after death of Coligny. Became first Bourbon king of France after converting to Catholicism, saying, "Paris is worth a mass." Issued Edict of Nantes in 1598 granting toleration to Huguenots. Was assassinated by Catholic fanatic in 1610.
PIERRE DU MOULIN	1568–1658	Pastor	Studied at Cambridge University. Taught at University of Leyden. Pastored Reformed church at Charenton for many years.
JEAN DAILLÉ	1594–1670	Theologian	Was educated at Saumur. Became chaplain to Duplessis-Mornay. Attacked authority of patristic writings. Supported Amyraldianism.
MOSES AMYRAUT	1596–1664	Theologian	Studied under Scotsman John Cameron at Saumur. Became professor at University of Saumur. Attempted compromise between Calvinism and Arminianism; it became known as Amyraldianism.
PIERRE JURIEU	1637–1713	Theologian	Studied at Saumur. Defended Reformed faith against critics. Believed Apocalypse predicted restoration of Huguenots. Advocated violent overthrow of Louis XIV. Was viewed as prophet by Camisards in War of the Cevennes.
ANTOINE COURT	1696–1760	Pastor	Led Church of the Desert during persecution of Louis XIV. Established seminary to train Huguenot ministers in Lausanne and operated it for 30 years. Carried on voluminous correspondence with Reformed leaders.
PAUL RABAUT	1718–1794	Pastor	Studied under Court in Lausanne. Ministered in hiding to Church of the Desert. Became recognized as leader of Reformed Protestants in France. Was instrumental in gaining eventual recognition for Protestants.

Chart 65

Church and State in France (1515–1589)

MONARCH AND DATES	YEARS OF REIGN	NOTABLE FACTS AND EVENTS
FRANCIS I (1494–1547)	1515–1547	1516 – Signed Concordat of Bologna with pope, giving king control over Gallican church. 1531 – Formed alliance with Protestant Smalcald League. 1536 – Began persecution of Huguenots. 1545 – Massacred inhabitants of several Waldensian villages.
HENRY II (1519–1559)	1547–1559	Son of Francis I 1533 – Married Catherine de Medici, by whom he was dominated. Persecuted Huguenots more severely than his father. 1555 – Failed Calvin – Coligny mission to Brazil 1559 – Huguenots produced Gallican Confession at National Synod in Paris. 1559 – Died after being wounded by a lance in the eye during a joust.
FRANCIS II (1544–1560)	1559–1560	Eldest son of Henry II and Catherine de Medici Married Mary Stuart in 1558. 1560 – Tumult of Amboise sought to overthrow the Catholic Guises, de facto rulers of the kingdom.
CHARLES IX (1550–1574)	1560–1574	Son of Henry II and Catherine de Medici 1561 – Colloquy of Poissy sought theological reconciliation between Catholics and Huguenots. 1562 – Huguenots massacred at Vassy, leading to the beginning of religious wars in France. 1563 – Peace of Amboise granted freedom of worship to Huguenot aristocrats. 1571 – Came under the influence of Huguenot leader Gaspard de Coligny. 1572 – Huguenot Henry of Navarre married Margaret of Valois, daughter of Henry II. 1572 – St. Bartholomew's Day Massacre resulted in slaughter of thousands of Huguenots, including Coligny.
HENRY III (1551–1589)	1574–1589	Son of Henry II and Catherine de Medici, by whom he was dominated 1576 – Huguenots granted freedom of worship except in Paris. 1589 – Formed alliance with Henry of Navarre against Guises. 1589 – Named Huguenot Henry of Navarre as his successor before being assassinated by a Catholic monk; died childless, ending Valois dynasty.

Chart 66

Protestant Creeds of the Reformation Era

CREED	DATE	CHURCH	COMPOSED BY	DISTINCTIVES	HISTORICAL NOTES
SCHLEITHEIM CONFESSION	1527	Swiss Anabaptist	Michael Sattler	Emphasized believers' baptism, strict church discipline, separation of church from state and believers from world, pacifism.	Not a formal creed. Rare example of Anabaptist summary of doctrine. Sattler martyred months after document was composed.
AUGSBURG CONFESSION	1530	German Lutheran	Philip Melanchthon Martin Luther	Emphasizes justification by faith. Opposes unbiblical Catholic practices. Condemns Anabaptists. Opposes Zwinglian view of Lord's Supper.	Drafted largely by Melanchthon, reviewed by Luther and others. Presented to Charles V at Diet of Augsburg; rejected. Became major Lutheran Confession.
TETRAPOLITAN CONFESSION	1530	German Reformed	Martin Bucer Wolfgang Capito	Similar to Augsburg Confession, but closer to Zwingli's views	Accepted only by cities of Strasbourg, Memmingen, Lindau, and Constance.
FIRST HELVETIC CONFESSION	1536	Swiss Reformed	Heinrich Bullinger Oswald Myconius	Zwinglian view of Lord's Supper, though it does speak of spiritual presence of Christ	Prepared by Swiss in an effort to bring about reconciliation with Lutherans.
ARTICLES OF SMALCALD	1537	German Lutheran	Martin Luther Philip Melanchthon	Emphasizes justification by faith. Strong anti-papal declarations	Prepared for council called by Paul III. Melanchthon argued that the pope could rightly oversee bishops if he permitted the gospel to be preached.
GALLICAN CONFESSION	1559	French Reformed (Huguenots)	John Calvin Antoine de Chandieu Theodore Beza	Basic summary of Calvin's teachings Introduced natural theology.	Drafted originally by Calvin, expanded by Huguenots. Accompanied by letter to Francis II seeking end of persecution.
SCOTS CONFESSION	1560	Scottish Presbyterian	John Knox and others	Calvinistic, similar to Gallican Confession	Written in four days, adopted immediately by Parliament. Replaced by Westminster Confession in 1647.
BELGIC CONFESSION	1561	Belgian Reformed	Guido de Brès	Further elaboration on Gallican Confession	Attempt by persecuted Protestants to prove Reformed faith from Scripture. Written during Spanish persecution in the Low Countries.

Chart 67

Protestant Creeds of the Reformation Era (continued)

CREED	DATE	CHURCH	COMPOSED BY	DISTINCTIVES	HISTORICAL NOTES
HEIDELBERG CATECHISM	1563	German Reformed	Caspar Olevianus Zacharias Ursinus	Contains elements of both Calvinist and Lutheran views.	Prepared at request of Frederick III, Elector Palatine. Later revised by Synod of Dordt.
THIRTY-NINE ARTICLES	1563	Anglican	Matthew Parker and others	Deliberately vague to be as inclusive as possible	Revision of earlier Forty-two Articles. Final alterations made by Elizabeth I personally.
SECOND HELVETIC CONFESSION	1566	Swiss Reformed	Heinrich Bullinger	Moderate statement of Reformed doctrine emphasizing continuity with ancient church teaching	Private confession of Bullinger, included in his will.
FORMULA OF CONCORD	1577	German Lutheran	Jacob Andreae Martin Chemnitz	Emphasizes bondage of the will, distinction between law and gospel, consubstantiation.	Prepared to settle disputes between followers of Luther and Melanchthon on free will and the presence of Christ in the Lord's Supper.
LAMBETH ARTICLES	1595	Anglican	John Whitgift	Calvinistic, supralapsarian	Never accepted by church. Repudiated by Elizabeth I.
CANONS OF DORDT	1619	Dutch Reformed	Delegates to Synod of Dordt	Formulated Five Points of Calvinism in response to Arminian Remonstrance.	Synod called in response to Arminian controversy. Included advisors from England, Scotland, and Germany.
WESTMINSTER CONFESSION	1647	English Presbyterian	Delegates to Westminster Assembly	First confession of faith to incorporate Covenant Theology explicitly; emphasizes Puritan Sabbath.	Attempt to provide a single confession for England and Scotland following Solemn League and Covenant.
SAVOY DECLARATION	1658	English Congregationalist	Thomas Goodwin, John Owen, and others	Congregationalist reworking of Westminster Confession; rejected role of civil government in punishing heresy.	Attempted to win recognition for Congregationalists alongside Presbyterians.
HELVETIC CONSENSUS	1675	Swiss Reformed	Francis Turretin John Heidegger	Opposed Amyraut's view of universal atonement. Opposed supralapsarianism. Asserted verbal inspiration of Scripture.	Swiss defense of Canons of Dordt against Amyraldianism. Rescinded by Swiss Church in 1725.
LONDON BAPTIST CONFESSION	1689	English Particular Baptist	Hanserd Knollys, William Kiffin, and others	Baptist reworking of Westminster Confession; changed sections on baptism and civil government.	Sought to distinguish Particular Baptists from General (Arminian) Baptists. Sought to exempt Baptists from persecution.

Chart 67

Leaders of the Catholic Counterreformation

NAME	DATES	HOME COUNTRY	EDUCATION	NOTABLE FACTS
TOMAS DE TORQUE-MADA	1420–1498	Spain	Valladolid	Became a Dominican monk. Was confessor of Ferdinand and Isabella. Was first Inquisitor-General of Spain. Was active in driving Jews and Moors from Spain.
FRANCISCO XIMENES	1436–1517	Spain	Salamanca	Was a prominent Spanish preacher. Entered Franciscan order. Was confessor of Queen Isabella. Became archbishop of Toledo, later cardinal. Founded University of Alcala. Oversaw printing of *Complutensian Polyglot Bible*.
GIOVANNI CARAFFA (Paul IV)	1476–1559	Italy	Naples	Became bishop of Chiete in 1506. Was papal envoy to England, Flanders, Spain. Helped found Theatines in 1524. Was made cardinal in 1536. Was pope 1555–1559. Initiated *Index of Prohibited Books*.
JACOPO SADOLETO	1477–1547	Italy	Pisa Ferraro Rome	Served as secretary to Leo X and Clement VII. Became cardinal with other Reformers in 1536. Corresponded with Melanchthon and Calvin, attempting to reconcile them to Catholic Church. His reform ideas were largely ignored by hierarchy.
GASPARO CONTARINI	1483–1542	Italy	Padua	Was appointed ambassador of Venice to England, Spain, Italy. Became cardinal in 1536. Attempted reconciliation with Protestants. Produced joint statement on justification with Melanchthon and Bucer at Regensburg in 1541.
IGNATIUS LOYOLA	1491–1556	Spain	Alcala Salamanca Paris	Was soldier, wounded and lamed in 1521. Entered Dominican order. Wrote *Spiritual Exercises*. Founded Society of Jesus in 1534. Founded Roman College in 1551.

Chart 68

Leaders of the Catholic Counterreformation (continued)

NAME	DATES	HOME COUNTRY	EDUCATION	NOTABLE FACTS
REGINALD POLE	1500–1558	England	Oxford Padua	Was exiled for opposition to Henry VIII's divorce. Became cardinal in 1536. Succeeded Cranmer as archbishop of Canterbury. Attempted to restore England to Catholicism under Mary Tudor.
MICHELE GHISLIERI (Pius V)	1504–1572	Italy	Bosco	Entered Dominican order. Headed Roman Inquisition. Became cardinal in 1557, pope in 1566. Encouraged destruction of Protestants in the Netherlands and France. Excommunicated Elizabeth I of England.
JAMES LAYNEZ	1512–1565	Spain	Alcala Paris	Was one of six original members of Society of Jesus. Preached forcefully against Protestantism. Later became head of Jesuits. Led papal party at Council of Trent, helped shape anti-Protestant canons.
TERESA OF ÁVILA	1515–1582	Spain	Augustinian convent in Ávila	Entered Carmelite convent in 1535, but began taking disciplines seriously in 1555, after which she began to have ecstatic visions. Founded Convent of St. Joseph in 1562 for strict Discalced (Barefoot) Carmelites. Wrote *The Way of Perfection.* Reached state of "spiritual marriage" with Christ in 1572.
PETER CANISIUS	1521–1597	Germany	Cologne	Entered Society of Jesus in 1543. Was a leader of Counterreformation in southern Germany. Wrote three catechisms, which were translated into 12 languages and widely disseminated.
CHARLES BORROMEO	1538–1584	Italy	Arona	Was named abbot of Arona monastery at age 12. Became cardinal in 1559, archbishop of Milan in 1560. Was an active reforming influence at Council of Trent. Founded many schools and orphanages.
JOHN OF THE CROSS	1542–1591	Spain	Salamanca	Entered Carmelite monastery in 1563, ordained to priesthood in 1567. Brought friars into Discalced Carmelite movement, encouraged by Teresa of Ávila. Imprisoned by Calced Carmelites 1577–1578. Wrote *Living Flame of Love.*
ROBERT BELLARMINE	1542–1621	Italy	Padua Louvain	Entered Society of Jesus in 1560. Became professor of theology at Louvain. Was the chief Catholic apologist of his age. Became cardinal in 1599. Opposed teachings of Galileo.

Chart 68

Religious Wars of the Reformation

WAR	DATES	LOCALITY	MAJOR PARTICIPANTS	KEY LEADERS	OUTCOME
PEASANTS' REVOLT	1524–1525	Germany	Peasants vs. nobility	Thomas Münzer Philip of Hesse	Brutal suppression of peasants Twelve Articles
KAPPEL WARS	1529, 1531	Switzerland	Catholic vs. Protestant cantons	Ulrich Zwingli	Death of Zwingli and defeat of Protestants
SMALCALD WAR	1546–1555	Germany	German Protestant princes vs. Holy Roman Emperor	Emperor Charles V Philip of Hesse John Frederick of Saxony Duke Maurice of Saxony	Defeat of Protestants Settlement of Interim Renewed hostilities Legal recognition of Lutherans Peace of Augsburg *Cuius Regio, Eius Religio*
DUTCH REVOLT	1559–1579	Netherlands	Spain vs. Netherlands	Philip II of Spain William the Silent	Netherlands divided by Protestant Union of Utrecht in north (Holland), Catholic League of Arras in south (Belgium)
FRENCH CIVIL WAR	1562–1593	France	Catholics vs. Huguenots	Gaspar de Coligny Henry of Navarre Philippe Duplessis-Mornay Catherine de Medici Henry of Guise Henry III	St. Bartholomew's Day Massacre (1572) Defeat of Huguenots Accession of Henry of Navarre to throne as Henry IV Edict of Nantes (1598)
THIRTY YEARS' WAR	1618–1648	Germany and Central Europe	Holy Roman Empire vs. Germany Denmark Sweden France Spain	Elector Palatine Frederick V Emperor Ferdinand Gustavus Adolphus Duke Maximilian of Bavaria Johan Tilly Christian IV Albrecht Wallenstein	Peace of Westphalia Political and religious boundaries fixed Limited religious toleration approved Jesuits excluded from Protestant lands Calvinism recognized
ENGLISH CIVIL WAR	1642–1648	England	Cavaliers (Royalists) vs. Roundheads (Parliamentary Army; Puritans)	Charles I Oliver Cromwell	Defeat of Royalists Execution of Charles I Exile of Stuart monarchy Formation of Commonwealth, followed by Protectorate

Chart 69

Theological Issues—Protestant versus Catholic

AREA	ISSUE	PROTESTANT POSITION	CATHOLIC POSITION
SCRIPTURE	SUFFICIENCY	Sola Scriptura	Tradition of equal authority with Scripture
	APOCRYPHA	Rejected	Accepted
ANTHROPOLOGY	ORIGINAL SIN	Total depravity and guilt inherited from Adam	Corruption and predisposition to evil inherited from Adam
	HUMAN WILL	In bondage to sin	Free to do spiritual good
SOTERIOLOGY	PREDESTINATION	Rooted in God's decrees	Rooted in God's foreknowledge
	ATONEMENT	Christ's death a substitutionary penal sacrifice	Christ's death the merit for blessings of salvation— blessings passed on to sinners through sacraments
	GRACE OF GOD	Common grace given to all; saving grace given to elect	Prevenient grace, given at baptism, enabling one to believe; efficacious grace cooperating with the will enabling one to obey
	GOOD WORKS	Produced by the grace of God, unworthy of merit of any kind	Meritorious
	REGENERATION	Work of the Holy Spirit in the elect	Grace infused at baptism
	JUSTIFICATION	Objective, final, judicial act of God	Forgiveness of sins received at baptism, may be lost by committing mortal sin, regained by penance
ECCLESIOLOGY	CHURCH AND SALVATION	Distinction between visible and invisible church	Outside the (visible) church there is no salvation
	SACRAMENTS	Means of grace only as received by faith	Conveying justifying and sanctifying grace *ex opere operato*
	PRIESTHOOD	All believers are priests	Mediators between God and man
	TRANSUBSTANTIA-TION	Rejected	Affirmed
ESCHATOLOGY	PURGATORY	Denied	Affirmed

Chart 70

Theological Issues—Lutheran versus Reformed

ISSUE	LUTHERAN POSITION	REFORMED POSITION
ORDO SALUTIS	Calling, illumination, conversion, regeneration, justification, sanctification, glorification	Election, predestination, union with Christ, calling, regeneration, faith, repentance, justification, sanctification, glorification
GRACE OF GOD	Grace received through baptism or preaching, enabling one to avoid resisting the regenerating grace of God	Irresistible
REPENTANCE	Leads to faith	Flows from faith
BAPTISM	Works regeneration, removing guilt and power of sin	Incorporation into the Covenant of Grace
LORD'S SUPPER	Christ present in the sacrament objectively	Sign and seal of the Covenant of Grace to believers; Christ present by faith
CHURCH AND STATE	State church to tutor in the faith the rulers who support Protestantism	Holy Commonwealth, in which church and state are both Christian, yet perform their separate functions
REGULATIVE PRINCIPLE	Whatever is not forbidden in Scripture is permissible	Whatever is not commanded in Scripture is forbidden

Chart 71

Theological Issues—Calvinist versus Arminian

ISSUE	CALVINIST POSITION	ARMINIAN POSITION
ORIGINAL SIN	Total depravity and guilt inherited from Adam	Weakness inherited from Adam
HUMAN WILL	In bondage to sin	Free to do spiritual good
GRACE OF GOD	Common grace given to all; saving grace given to elect	Enabling grace given to all; saving grace given to those who believe; persevering grace given to those who obey
PREDESTINATION	Rooted in God's decrees	Rooted in God's foreknowledge
REGENERATION	Monergistic	Synergistic
ATONEMENT	Christ's death a substitutionary penal sacrifice	Christ's death a sacrifice that God benevolently accepted in place of a penalty
EXTENT OF ATONEMENT	Intended only for the elect	Intended for all
APPLICATION OF ATONEMENT	By power of the Holy Spirit according to the will of God	By power of the Holy Spirit in response to the will of the sinner
ORDO SALUTIS	Election, predestination, union with Christ, calling, regeneration, faith, repentance, justification, sanctification, glorification	Calling, faith, repentance, regeneration, justification, perseverance, glorification
PERSEVERANCE	Perseverance of all the elect by the grace of God	Perseverance dependent on obedience

Chart 72

A Family Tree of Protestant Denominational Groups

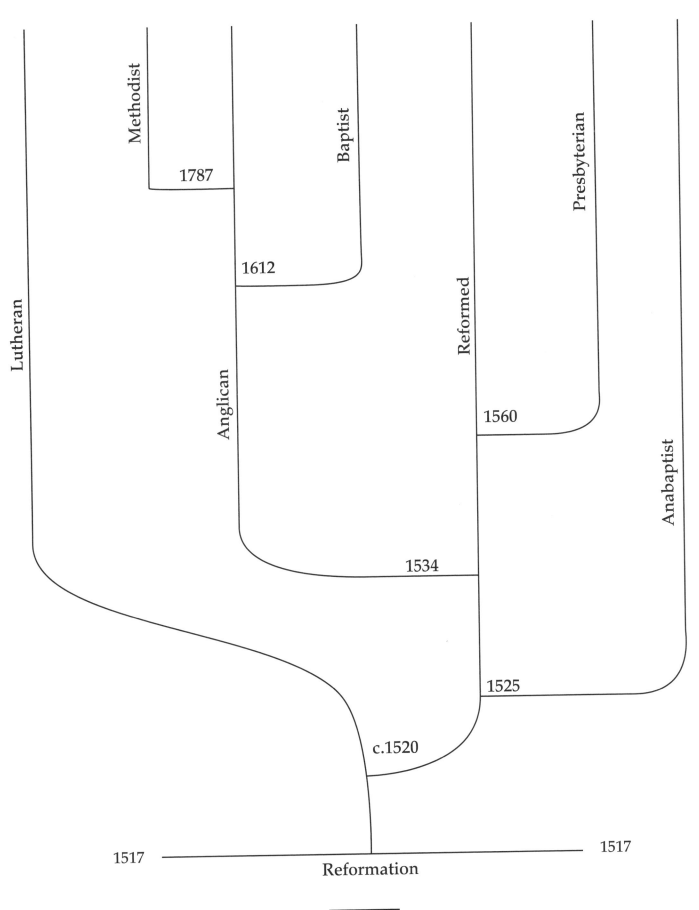

Lutheran

Methodist

1787

Baptist

Anglican

1612

Reformed

Presbyterian

1560

1534

Anabaptist

1525

c.1520

1517 —— Reformation —— 1517

Chart 73

THE
MODERN CHURCH
(FROM 1648)

A Timeline of the Modern Church in Britain (from 1688)

	1650 AD–1680 AD	1680 AD–1710 AD	1710 AD–1740 AD	1740 AD–1770 AD	1770 AD–1800 AD
PEOPLE	John Locke (1632–1704) Matthew Tindal (1655–1733) Thomas Bray (1656–1730) John Toland (1670–1722) Isaac Watts (1674–1748) Anthony Collins (1676–1729) Thomas Boston (1676–1732) Ebenezer Erskine (1680–1754)	William Law (1686–1761) Joseph Butler (1692–1752) William Warburton (1698–1779) John Wesley (1703–1791) Charles Wesley (1707–1788) Selina Hastings (1707–1791)	Daniel Rowland (c.1713–1790) George Whitefield (1714–1770) Howell Harris (1714–1773) William Williams (1717–1791) John Newton (1725–1807) John Howard (1726–1790) William Paley (1743–1805) Robert Raikes (1735–1811) Granville Sharp (1735–1813)	William Wilberforce (1759–1833) William Carey (1761–1834) Robert Haldane (1764–1842) Christmas Evans (1766–1838)	John Elias (1774–1841) Thomas Chalmers (1780–1847) Henry Martyn (1781–1812) Robert Morrison (1782–1834) John Keble (1792–1866) Robert Moffat (1795–1883) John Nelson Darby (1800–1882)
EVENTS		Glorious Revolution (1688) London Baptist Confession (1689)	Salters' Hall Meeting (1719) Aldersgate Street meeting (1738)	Handel's *Messiah* (1741)	American Revolution (1776–1783) Carey leaves for India (1793) Methodist Church founded (1795)

Chart 74

A Timeline of the Modern Church in Britain (from 1688), continued

	1800 AD–1830 AD	1830 AD–1860 AD	1860 AD–1890 AD	1890 AD–1920 AD	1920 AD–1950 AD
PEOPLE	A. A. Cooper, 7th Earl of Shaftesbury (1801–1885) John Henry Newman (1801–1890) George Müller (1805–1898) Alexander Duff (1806–1878) Horatius Bonar (1808–1889) David Livingstone (1813–1873) Robert Murray McCheyne (1814–1843) George MacDonald (1824–1905) John G. Paton (1824–1907) William Booth (1829–1912)	Hudson Taylor (1832–1905) Charles H. Spurgeon (1834–1892) Mary Slessor (1848–1915)	C. T. Studd (1862–1931) G. Campbell Morgan (1863–1945) Amy Carmichael (1867–1951) Oswald Chambers (1874–1917) G. K. Chesterton (1874–1936) Evan Roberts (1878–1951) William Temple (1881–1944) A. W. Pink (1886–1952)	J. R. R. Tolkien (1892–1973) Dorothy L. Sayers (1893–1957) C. S. Lewis (1898–1963) D. Martyn Lloyd-Jones (1899–1981) F. F. Bruce (1910–1990)	John Stott (b.1921) J. I. Packer (b.1926)
EVENTS		Tractarian Movement begins (1833) Darwin's *The Origin of Species* (1859)	Salvation Army founded (1865)		

Chart 74

A Timeline of the Modern Church in Germany (from 1648)

	1650 AD–1680 AD	1680 AD–1710 AD	1710 AD–1740 AD	1740 AD–1770 AD	1770 AD–1800 AD
PEOPLE	Philipp Jakob Spener (1635–1705) Gottfried von Leibniz (1646–1716) Joachim Neander (1650–1680) Auguste H. Francke (1663–1727) Alexander Mack (1679–1735)	Bartholomaus Ziegen-balg (1684–1719) J. A. Bengel (1687–1752) Nikolaus von Zinzendorf (1700–1760) August Spangenberg (1704–1792)	Peter Boehler (1712–1775) Immanuel Kant (1724–1804) Christian F. Schwartz (1726–1798)	Friedrich Schleierm-acher (1768–1834) G. W. F. Hegel (1770–1831)	J. A. W. Neander (1789–1850) F. C. Baur (1792–1860)
EVENTS	Spener's *Pia Desideria* (1675)		Herrnhut founded (1722)		

Chart 75

A Timeline of the Modern Church in Germany (from 1648), continued

	1800 AD–1830 AD	1830 AD–1860 AD	1860 AD–1890 AD	1890 AD–1920 AD	1920 AD–1950 AD
PEOPLE	E. W. Hengstenberg (1802–1869) Johann Keil (1807–1888) David F. Strauss (1808–1874) Johann Krapf (1810–1881) Franz Delitzsch (1813–1890) Constantin von Tischendorf (1815–1874) Johannes Rebmann (1819–1876) Albrecht Ritschl (1822–1889)	Friedrich Nietzsche (1844–1900) Julius Wellhausen (1844–1918) Adolf von Harnack (1851–1930)	Ernst Troeltsch (1865–1923) Albert Schweitzer (1875–1965) Rudolf Bultmann (1884–1976) Paul Tillich (1886–1965) Karl Barth (1886–1968)	Karl Rahner (1904–1984) Dietrich Bonhoeffer (1906–1945)	Jürgen Moltmann (b.1926) Wolfhart Pannenberg (b.1928) Hans Küng (b.1928)
EVENTS		Tischendorf discovers *Codex Sinaiticus* (1844)	Unification of Germany (1870)		Barmen Declaration (1934)

Chart 75

A Timeline of the Modern Church in France, Switzerland, and the Netherlands (from 1648)

		1650 AD–1680 AD	1680 AD–1710 AD	1710 AD–1740 AD	1740 AD–1770 AD	1770 AD–1800 AD
PEOPLE	**FRANCE**	Pierre Jurieu (1637–1713)	Atoine Court (1696–1760) Jean Calas (d.1762)	Paul Rabaut (1718–1794) Rabaut St. Etienne (d.1794)		Frederick Monod (1794–1863)
	SWITZERLAND	Francis Turretin (b.1623)				César Malan (1787–1864) François Gaussen (1790–1863) J. H. Merle d'Aubigne (1794–1872)
	NETHERLANDS				Robert Haldane (1764–1842)	Isaak da Costa (1798–1860)
EVENTS	**FRANCE**		Edict of Nantes revoked (1685) Camisard War (1703–1711)	Papal bull against Jansenists (1713)		Edict of Toleration (1787) Civil Constitution of the Clergy (1790)
	SWITZERLAND	Helvetic Consensus (1675)		Helvetic Consensus revoked (1725)		
	NETHERLANDS					

Chart 76

A Timeline of the Modern Church in France, Switzerland, and the Netherlands (from 1648) cont.

		1800 AD–1830 AD	1830 AD–1860 AD	1860 AD–1890 AD	1890 AD–1920 AD
PEOPLE	FRANCE	Adolphe Monod (1802–1856) Charles Lavigerie (1825–1892)	Charles de Foucauld (1858–1916)	Pierre Teilhard de Chardin (1881–1955)	
	SWITZERLAND	Frederic Godet (1812–1900) Philip Schaff (1819–1893)		Karl Barth (1886–1968) Emil Brunner (1889–1966)	
	NETHERLANDS	Groen van Prinsterer (c.1800–1867)	Abraham Kuyper (1837–1920)		Herman Dooyeweerd (1894–1977)
EVENTS	FRANCE	Concordat signed with the pope (1801)			
	SWITZERLAND		Reformed Seminary of Geneva founded (1834)		
	NETHERLANDS			Free University of Amsterdam founded (1880)	Kuyper serves as prime minister (1901–1905)

Chart 76

Leaders in the Development of Science and Their Relationship to the Church

SCIENTIST	DATES	COUNTRY	SCIENTIFIC CONTRIBUTIONS	RELATIONSHIP TO CHURCH
NICHOLAS COPERNICUS	1473–1543	Poland	Developed heliocentric theory of solar system based on Ockham's Razor. Wrote *On the Revolution of the Heavenly Orbs* in 1543.	Devout Catholic Contemporary of Luther, who referred to him as "that fool who would overthrow the entire science of astronomy." Book put on *Index of Forbidden Books* by Council of Trent.
FRANCIS BACON	1561–1626	England	Developed the Scientific Method, though he failed to appreciate the importance of mathematics to science. Wrote *Novum Organum* in 1620.	Orthodox Anglican Served as Lord Chancellor of England under James I, lost position after conviction for bribery and corruption. Believed that science and theology should be kept separate.
GALILEO GALILEI	1564–1642	Italy	Improved telescope. Discovered sunspots, moons of Jupiter. Laid groundwork for Newton's work on motion.	Support of heliocentric theory led to condemnation for heresy by the Inquisition in 1632; he was forced to recant and spent the last ten years of his life under house arrest.
JOHANN KEPLER	1571–1630	Germany	Formulated three laws of planetary motion that put the heliocentric theory on a firm mathematical footing.	Lutheran mystic; his view that the universe was an emanation of God favored pantheism. Supported his scientific studies by casting horoscopes.
RENÉ DESCARTES	1596–1650	France	Developed coordinate geometry. Sought to make mathematics the basis for philosophy. Rationalism—*cogito ergo sum*.	Studied under Jesuits, but saw little value in what they taught him. Incorporated Ontological Argument for the existence of God into his philosophical system to avoid the attention of the Inquisition.
BLAISE PASCAL	1623–1662	France	Developed theory of probability. Invented calculating machine. Did work in fluid dynamics.	Converted by Jansenists at age 31. Devoted remainder of his life to writing apologetic for Christianity; unfinished at his death, it was collected and published as *Pensées*. Attacked Jesuit casuistry in his *Lettres Provinciales*. Opposed Descartes' Rationalism.
ROBERT BOYLE	1627–1691	Ireland	Formulated Boyle's Law. Helped found Royal Society in 1660.	Converted at age 14 after severe storm. Encouraged by many to enter ministry, but believed his testimony in the scientific community would be more valuable. Used wealth to support missionary work and Bible distribution. Wrote a devotional book, *Seraphic Love*, in 1660. Endowed Boyle Lectures to defend intellecual credibility of Christianity.

Chart 77

SCIENTIST	DATES	COUNTRY	SCIENTIFIC CONTRIBUTIONS	RELATIONSHIP TO CHURCH
ISAAC NEWTON	1642–1727	England	Formulated three laws of motion, law of gravity. Divided white light into component colors. Developed corpuscular theory of light. Invented calculus. President of Royal Society. Wrote *Principia Mathematica*.	Convinced that science could lead to a better understanding of God's world. Wrote many theological works later in life, though his theology was suspect because of Arian tendencies. Supported charitable societies and Bible distribution. Mathematical formulations laid groundwork for Deism and its idea of a great World Machine.
GOTTFRIED WILHELM VON LEIBNIZ	1646–1716	Germany	Developed calculus at the same time as Newton; the two spent the rest of their lives fighting over who had done it first.	Saw Christianity as the sum of truth found in all religions. Sought to unify Protestants and Catholics after carnage of Thirty Years' War. Saw this world as "the best of all possible worlds." Wrote theological and philosophical works.
JOSEPH PRIESTLEY	1733–1804	England	Discovered oxygen.	Rejected central doctrines of the Christian faith. Driven from England in 1794 for supporting the French Revolution. Became pastor of the first Unitarian church in Pennsylvania.
MICHAEL FARADAY	1791–1867	England	Discovered electromagnetic induction and laws of electrolysis. Developed electric motor, dynamo, transformer.	Strongly evangelical; belonged to Sandemanian sect. Used science to demonstrate truth of God and Scripture. Used all his wealth to promote Christian causes.
CHARLES DARWIN	1809–1882	England	Developed theory of evolution. Wrote *The Origin of Species* (1859) and *The Descent of Man* (1871).	Originally intended to enter Anglican ministry, but later turned to agnosticism. Theory of evolution was basis for much of the anti-Christian science, philosophy, and social theory of the 20th century.
ASA GRAY	1810–1888	United States	Leading American botanist of the 19th century. Wrote *Synoptical Flora* in 1878.	Evangelical Christian who opposed Darwin's theory through extensive correspondence. Accepted microevolution but not macroevolution.
WILLIAM THOMSON, LORD KELVIN	1824–1907	Northern Ireland	Developed Second Law of Thermodynamics. Calculated absolute zero, thus providing the basis for the Kelvin scale. Played key role in laying of transatlantic cable.	Committed Christian who opposed evolution on both biblical and scientific grounds; convinced that Darwin's theory required an undirected, massive, long-term violation of the Second Law of Thermodynamics.
JAMES CLERK MAXWELL	1831–1879	Scotland	Published scientific papers in his teens. Developed kinetic theory of gases. Developed electromagnetic theory.	Convinced that his scientific work repeatedly confirmed the Christian faith to which he was committed.

Chart 77

English Deism and Its Opponents

	NAME	DATES	REPRESENTATIVE WRITINGS	CONTRIBUTIONS TO DEBATE
FORERUNNERS OF DEISM	THOMAS HOBBES	1588–1679	*Leviathan* *Behemoth*	All knowledge derived from senses and reason. Scripture is not contrary to reason. Existence attributed to material only.
	JOHN LOCKE	1632–1704	*The Reasonableness of Christianity* *Essay Concerning Human Understanding*	Revelation cannot contradict reason. Taught the idea of the *tabula rasa*. Knowledge comes by reflection on sensations.
	ISAAC NEWTON	1642–1727	*Principia Mathematica*	His picture of a mechanistic universe was eagerly seized by Deists.
LEADING DEISTS	EDWARD HERBERT, LORD CHERBURY	1583–1648	*De Veritate*	Was influenced by Montaigne. Supernatural revelation is not necessary for religion.
	MATTHEW TINDAL	1655–1733	*Christianity as Old as the Creation*	Asserted absolute sufficiency of natural religion. Taught that Christianity is to be tested by natural religion. Declared that creation is perfect, so nothing can or should be added to it.
	THOMAS WOOLSTON	1669–1733	*Six Discourses on the Miracles of Our Savior*	Insisted that New Testament miracles were symbolic, not factual. Affirmed that the Resurrection was a hoax perpetrated by disciples.
	JOHN TOLAND	1670–1722	*Christianity Not Mysterious*	Denied that Christianity introduced anything not previously known.
	ANTHONY COLLINS	1676–1729	*A Discourse on Free Thinking* *Discourse on the Grounds and Reasons of the Christian Religion*	Since biblical writers were freethinkers, so should we be. There is no real correspondence between Old Testament prophecies and the life of Christ.

Chart 78

English Deism and Its Opponents (continued)

<table>
<tr><td rowspan="6" style="writing-mode: vertical">APOLOGISTS AGAINST DEISM</td><td></td><td>NAME</td><td>DATES</td><td>REPRESENTATIVE WRITINGS</td><td>CONTRIBUTIONS TO DEBATE</td></tr>
</table>

	NAME	DATES	REPRESENTATIVE WRITINGS	CONTRIBUTIONS TO DEBATE
APOLOGISTS AGAINST DEISM	GEORGE BERKELEY	1685–1753	*Alciphron*	Attributed a real existence to God's ideas, not to matter.
	WILLIAM LAW	1686–1761	*The Case of Reason* *A Serious Call to a Devout and Holy Life*	Attempted to refute Tindal's arguments. Declared that God's actions are not always according to human reason. His devotional works strongly influenced John Wesley.
	JOSEPH BUTLER	1692–1752	*Analogy of Religion*	Was greatest opponent of Deism. His *Analogy* was used as an apologetics text for 200 years. Taught that natural religion is insufficient without complementary revelation. Said that probable truth of revealed religion is as strong as probable truth of natural religion.
	WILLIAM WARBURTON	1698–1779	*The Divine Legation of Moses* *Principles of Natural and Revealed Religion*	Attempted to demonstrate divine origin of the Old Testament on basis of its lack of teaching on the afterlife. Argued that the Bible must be inspired because it goes against human reason.
	WILLIAM PALEY	1743–1805	*View of the Evidences of Christianity* *Natural Theology*	Gave lucid expression to anti-Deist apologetic. Gave classical form of teleological argument for the existence of God (the Watchmaker Argument).

Chart 78

Church and State in France (1589–1814)

MONARCH AND DATES	YEARS OF REIGN	NOTABLE FACTS AND EVENTS
HENRY IV (1553–1610)	1589–1610	1593 – Converted to Catholicism to secure throne. 1598 – Edict of Nantes granted toleration to Huguenots. 1600 – Married Marie de Medici. 1610 – Assassinated by Catholic fanatic.
LOUIS XIII (1601–1643)	1610–1643	Son of Henry IV and Marie de Medici, who controlled him in the early years of his reign. Cardinal Richelieu dominated public policy from 1624. 1621–1628 – "Huguenot Wars" 1628 – Fall of Huguenot fortress at La Rochelle 1629 – Peace of Alais deprives Huguenots of political and military power but not religious liberty. 1630 – France joins Protestant side in Thirty Years' War.
LOUIS XIV (1638–1715)	1643–1715	Son of Louis XIII and Anne of Austria Cardinal Mazarin dominated public policy until the king's majority. 1648 – Fronde rebellion of nobility against Cardinal Mazarin 1652 – Confirmed Edict of Nantes. 1660–1685 – Increased harassment of Huguenots. 1670 – Treaty of Dover offered money to Charles II of England in exchange for support of Catholicism. 1685 – Edict of Nantes revoked; thousands of Huguenots fled country. 1703–1711 – Camisard War in the Cevennes mountains 1711 – Jansenist center established at Port Royal 1713 – Papal bull Unigenitus against Jansenists
LOUIS XV (1710–1774)	1715–1774	Great-grandson of Louis XIV Duke of Orleans served as regent early in reign; later Cardinal Fleury controlled policy. 1726 – All Protestants condemned to slavery or imprisonment. 1752 – Unigenitus no longer enforced. 1764 – Jesuits suppressed.
LOUIS XVI (1754–1793)	1774–1792	Grandson of Louis XV 1770 – Married Marie Antoinette of Austria. 1787 – Edict of Toleration grants Huguenots freedom of worship. 1789 – French Revolution began. 1789 – Tithes abolished. 1790 – Monasteries dissolved. 1790 – Civil Constitution of the Clergy; condemned by the pope. 1793 – Louis XVI and Marie Antoinette guillotined.
REPUBLIC	1792–1804	1793–1794 – Reign of Terror 1793 – Hébertists initiate program of dechristianization; replace week with décade. 1794 – Cult of the Supreme Being established. 1801 – Concordat signed with the pope by Napoleon. 1802 – Protestant ministers as well as Catholic priests to be paid by state.
NAPOLEON I (1769–1821)	1804–1814	1804 – Napoleon declared emperor. 1808 – Napoleon excommunicated by the pope. 1808–1813 – Pope imprisoned by Napoleon. 1813 – Concordat of Fontainebleau signed by the pope under duress.

Chart 79

German Pietism and English Methodism—A Comparison

	PIETISM	METHODISM
FOUNDER	Philipp Jakob Spener (1635–1705)	John Wesley (1703–1791)
RELIGIOUS SITUATION	Stagnant orthodoxy of post-Reformation scholastic Lutheranism	Rationalistic Deism of post-Puritan Anglicanism
FOUNDATIONAL BOOK	Spener, *Pia Desideria*	William Law, *A Serious Call to a Devout and Holy Life*
EDUCATIONAL CENTER	University of Halle	Oxford University
ORGANIZATION	Conventicles	Methodist societies
OTHER KEY FIGURES	Auguste H. Francke (1663–1727) J. A. Bengel (1687–1752) Nikolaus von Zinzendorf (1700–1760) Peter Boehler (1712–1775) Alexander Mack (1679–1735)	Charles Wesley (1707–1788) George Whitefield (1714–1770) Thomas Coke (1747–1814) Francis Asbury (1745–1816) Selina Hastings, Countess of Huntingdon (1707–1791)
RESULTING CHURCHES	Church of the Brethren Moravian Church	Methodist Church Calvinistic Methodists (Countess of Huntingdon's Connexion)
COMMON EMPHASES	Practical holiness Personal Bible study Need for conscious conversion Evangelistic preaching Devotional exercises Relief of poor and needy Experience more than doctrine	
PIETIST INFLUENCES ON METHODISM	Wesleys met Moravians on ship to Georgia, were impressed with their quiet confidence (1735). Moravian Augustus Spangenberg questioned John Wesley in Georgia. John Wesley sought out Moravians in London; Boehler was instrumental in his conversion (1738). John Wesley visited Zinzendorf at Herrnhut (1738). Methodist societies were established, based on model of Pietist conventicles (1738).	

Chart 80

John Wesley and George Whitefield—A Contrast

	WESLEY	WHITEFIELD
PARENTAGE	Son of an Anglican rector in Epworth	Son of a tavern-keeper in Gloucester
EARLY LIFE	Strict religious upbringing supervised by mother, Susanna	Raised surrounded by worldly influences by mother, Elizabeth, who was widowed when George was two
CONVERSION	Aldersgate Street, London, at age 35	Oxford University, at age 21
ORDINATION	Church of England, 1728, at age 25	Church of England, 1736, at age 22
PREACHING STYLE	Intellectual, doctrinal	Dramatic, emotional
DOCTRINE	Arminian (though closer to Pietist semi-Augustinianism than to Dutch Arminianism)	Calvinistic
ORGANIZATIONAL ABILITY	Exceptional organizer; maintained personal control over total organization of Methodist societies.	Not a good organizer; preferred to preach and leave organizing to others.
MINISTRY OUTSIDE ENGLAND	Did early unsuccessful missionary work in Georgia; later preached in Scotland and Ireland; appointed bishops to supervise work in America.	Visited Scotland 14 times, participating in Cambuslang revival; visited America 7 times, becoming catalyst of First Great Awakening.
LEGACY	Methodist Church	Calvinistic Methodists; influence on Evangelical Party in Church of England

Chart 81

Other European Revivals

LOCATION	TIME	LEADING REVIVALISTS	RESULTING ORGANIZATIONS
WALES	Mid 18th century	Howell Harris (1714–1773) Daniel Rowland (c.1713–1790) William Williams (1717–1791)	
	Early 19th century	Christmas Evans (1766–1838) John Elias (1774–1841)	Calvinistic Methodist Church of Wales
	Early 20th century	Evan Roberts (1878–1951)	
SCOTLAND	Early to mid 19th century	Robert Haldane (1764–1842) James Haldane (1768–1851) Thomas Chalmers (1780–1847) Robert Murray McCheyne (1814–1843)	Society for the Propagation of the Gospel at Home Free Church of Scotland
SWITZERLAND	Early to mid 19th century	Robert Haldane (1764–1842) César Malan (1787–1864) François Gaussen (1790–1863) J. H. Merle D'Aubigné (1794–1863)	Evangelical Society of Geneva Evangelical Seminary in Geneva
FRANCE	Early to mid 19th century	Frederick Monod (1794–1863) Adolphe Monod (1802–1856)	Union of Evangelical Churches of France Archives du Christianisme
NETHERLANDS	Late 19th century	Groen van Prinsterer (c.1800–1867) Abraham Kuyper (1837–1920)	Free Reformed Church of the Netherlands Free University of Amsterdam

Chart 82

Evangelical Social Reformers in England

NAME	DATES	AREAS OF SOCIAL CONCERN	NOTABLE FACTS
JOHN NEWTON	1725–1807	Abolition of slavery	Was a sailor on slave ship. Became Anglican minister. Wrote many hymns, including "Amazing Grace." Influenced Wilberforce against slavery.
JOHN HOWARD	1726–1790	Prison reform	Was imprisoned by pirates in France. Wrote *State of the Prisons.* His impact extended throughout Europe.
ROBERT RAIKES	1735–1811	Education of urban poor	Was a newspaper publisher. Popularized the Sunday school. Was encouraged by John Wesley.
GRANVILLE SHARP	1735–1813	Abolition of slavery	Was associated with Clapham Sect. Stimulated founding of Sierra Leone. His work led to emancipation of slaves in England in 1772.
WILLIAM WILBERFORCE	1759–1833	Abolition of slavery	Was greatest British abolitionist. Became a member of Clapham Sect. Served many years in Parliament. Helped found British and Foreign Bible Society and Church Missionary Society. His work led to abolition of slave trade (1807) and emancipation of slaves throughout British Empire (1833).
A. A. COOPER, SEVENTH EARL OF SHAFTESBURY	1801–1885	Humane treatment of insane Reform of labor laws	Served many years in Parliament. Headed Lunacy Commission. Promoted passage of female and child labor laws.
GEORGE MÜLLER	1805–1898	Care of orphans	Was a member of Plymouth Brethren. Founded faith orphanage in Bristol but never solicited contributions for it. Was influenced by Pietist A. H. Francke.
WILLIAM BOOTH	1829–1912	Urban poverty	Was a Methodist minister. Wrote *In Darkest England* and *The Way Out.* Founded Salvation Army.

Chart 83

Major Figures in German Liberal Theology

NAME	DATES	REPRESENTATIVE WRITINGS	NOTABLE FACTS
FRIEDRICH SCHLEIERMACHER	1768–1834	*On Religion: Speeches to Its Cultured Despisers* *The Christian Faith*	Was raised in Pietist family. Attended University of Halle, later taught there and at University of Berlin. Rooted religion in feeling of absolute dependence. Theology coincided with Romantic movement in literature.
F. C. BAUR	1792–1860	*Paul the Apostle of Jesus Christ*	Taught at University of Tübingen. Applied Hegelian dialectic to New Testament, postulating Petrine and Pauline antitheses leading to Old Catholic synthesis. Denied authenticity of most of the New Testament.
DAVID FRIEDRICH STRAUSS	1808–1874	*Life of Jesus* *The Old and the New Faith*	Studied under Baur at Tübingen. Denied historicity of almost everything in the Gospels. Radical ideas cost him his teaching career. Eventually abandoned Christianity for "religion of humanity."
ALBRECHT RITSCHL	1822–1889	*The Christian Doctrine of Justification and Reconciliation* *Theology and Metaphysics*	Studied under Baur at Tübingen. Taught at Bonn and Göttingen. Rejected metaphysics. Emphasized ethical and social dimensions of Christianity. Pioneered "theology of moral value."
JULIUS WELLHAUSEN	1844–1918	*History of Israel*	Studied and taught at Göttingen. Originated Documentary Hypothesis, postulating that Pentateuch came from four anonymous sources referred to as J, E, D, and P.
ADOLF VON HARNACK	1851–1930	*What Is Christianity?* *History of Dogma* *The Mission and Expansion of Christianity in the First Three Centuries*	Was ancient church historian. Promulgated Social Gospel (fatherhood of God and brotherhood of man). Taught at University of Berlin.

Chart 84

Major Figures in German Liberal Theology (continued)

NAME	DATES	REPRESENTATIVE WRITINGS	NOTABLE FACTS
ERNST TROELTSCH	1865–1923	*The Absoluteness of Christianity* *Christian Thought, Its History and Application*	Taught at Göttingen, Bonn, Heidelberg, and Berlin. Believed that all religions were the product of history and culture. Denied that theology could have access to absolute truth. Believed that Christianity was the religion best suited to Western culture.
ALBERT SCHWEITZER	1875–1965	*The Quest of the Historical Jesus*	Earned doctorates in theology, medicine, and music. Was a missionary to Africa. Received Nobel Peace Prize (1952). Taught that Jesus mistakenly believed the end of the world was near.
RUDOLF BULTMANN	1884–1976	*Kerygma and Myth* *Theology of the New Testament* *Jesus and the Word* *The Form of the Synoptic Tradition*	Was an existentialist New Testament scholar. Was noted for "demythologizing" New Testament accounts. Taught at University of Marburg. Pioneered Form Criticism.
PAUL TILLICH	1886–1965	*Dynamics of Faith* *Systematic Theology* *The Courage to Be*	Was existentialist theologian. Was forced out of Germany under Hitler. Taught at Union Seminary in New York, Columbia, Harvard, and University of Chicago. Saw God as Ground of Being and faith as Ultimate Concern.
KARL BARTH	1886–1968	*Church Dogmatics* *Commentary on the Epistle to the Romans*	Was a Swiss theologian, founder of Neo-Orthodoxy. Broke from traditional liberalism in which he had been educated. Was the author of the Barmen Declaration. Was ousted from Germany for opposition to Hitler. His teachings included absolute transcendence of God, Bible's becoming the Word of God as it is read, and election of all people in Christ.

Chart 84

NAME	DATES	REPRESENTATIVE WRITINGS	NOTABLE FACTS
KARL RAHNER	1904–1984	*Spirit in the World*	Leading 20th century Roman Catholic theologian. Entered Jesuit order in 1922, ordained in 1932. Taught at Innsbruck and Munich. Played key role in Second Vatican Council. Influenced by Joseph Maréchal and existentialism of Martin Heidegger.
DIETRICH BONHOEFFER	1906–1945	*The Cost of Discipleship* *Letters and Papers from Prison*	Studied under Harnack and Barth. Helped draft the Barmen Declaration. Was a leader in the Confessing Church. Had mystical tendencies. Was executed in a Nazi concentration camp for involvement in a plot to assassinate Hitler.
JÜRGEN MOLTMANN	b.1926	*Theology of Hope* *The Crucified God* *The Church in the Power of the Spirit*	Raised in non-Christian home. Converted in Allied POW camp in Belgium during World War II. Taught at Bonn and Tübingen. Approach variously known as Theology of Hope, Theology of the Kingdom of God, and Liberation Theology.
WOLFHART PANNENBERG	b.1928	*Revelation as History* *Theology and the Philosophy of Science* *Systematic Theology*	Baptized Lutheran as a child, but raised in nonreligious environment. Taught theology at Heidelberg, Mainz, and Munich. Influenced by Barth and Moltmann. Emphasized knowing God through his self-disclosure in history.
HANS KÜNG	b.1928	*Council and Reunion* *Infallible? An Inquiry*	Swiss Roman Catholic theologian Taught at University of Tübingen. Involved in Second Vatican Council. Questioning of papal infallibility led John Paul II to revoke his teaching credentials. Described biblical accounts of life of Jesus as "nonhistorical events."

Chart 84

Other Prominent Figures in European Theology

NAME	DATES	COUNTRY	REPRESENTATIVE WRITINGS	NOTABLE FACTS
ROBERT HALDANE	1764–1842	Scotland	*Exposition of the Epistle to the Romans*	Prevented by British East India Company from going to India as a missionary. Used considerable fortune to build independent chapels throughout Scotland. Conducted Home Bible College in Geneva, led evangelical revival there.
FRANÇOIS GAUSSEN	1790–1863	Switzerland	*Theopneustia*	Leader in evangelical movement in Geneva. Founder of Evangelical Society. Deposed from pastorate and forbidden to preach because of his evangelical views.
JOHN HENRY NEWMAN	1801–1890	England	*Tracts of the Times* *Apologia pro Vita Sua*	Raised as an evangelical. Leader of Tractarian Movement, also known as Oxford or High Church Movement. Converted to Catholicism in 1845, became a cardinal in 1879.
E. W. HENGSTENBERG	1802–1869	Germany	*Christology of the Old Testament*	Taught at University of Berlin, where he faced opposition for rejecting higher criticism. Edited *Evangelische Lutherische Kirchenzeitung.*
JOHANN KEIL	1807–1888	Germany	*Commentaries on the Old Testament*	Taught at Dorpat (Estonia). Opposed higher criticism of Scripture. Collaborated with Delitzsch on OT commentary, also wrote commentaries on NT books.
SØREN KIERKEGAARD	1813–1855	Denmark	*Either-Or* *Fear and Trembling*	Studied theology at University of Copenhagen. Opposed deadness of established church. Forerunner of Neo-Orthodoxy and existentialism
FRANZ DELITZSCH	1813–1890	Germany	*Commentaries on the Old Testament* *Translation of the New Testament into Hebrew*	Jewish ancestry Taught at universities in Leipzig, Rostock, and Erlangen. Founded Jewish Missionary College in 1877.
J. ERNEST RENAN	1823–1892	France	*Life of Jesus* *History of the Origins of Christianity*	Left seminary just before ordination because he had lost his faith. Denied deity of Christ and historicity of biblical narratives. Named director of Collège de France after earlier being thrown out for heresy.
ABRAHAM KUYPER	1837–1920	Netherlands	*Calvinism* *The Work of the Holy Spirit*	Converted to orthodox Calvinism through influence of members of his country parish. Supported orthodoxy in opposition to the liberalism of the day. Founder of the Free University of Amsterdam. Served in Dutch States-General, was Prime Minister of the Netherlands 1901–1905.

Chart 85

NAME	DATES	COUNTRY	REPRESENTATIVE WRITINGS	NOTABLE FACTS
HERMAN BAVINCK	1854–1921	Netherlands	*Reformed Dogmatics* *Christian Philosophy*	Taught theology and apologetics at the Free University of Amsterdam 1902–1921. Conservative, confessional when much of the church around him was deviating from a confessional stance
PIERRE TEILHARD DE CHARDIN	1881–1955	France	*The Phenomenon of Man*	Jesuit philosopher, theologian, and anthropologist Involved in discovery of Peking Man and in Piltdown Man fiasco. Believed evolution would lead man to Omega Point and union with God.
EMIL BRUNNER	1889–1966	Switzerland	*Dogmatics* *The Divine-Human Encounter*	Neo-Orthodox theologian who opposed both orthodox theology and liberalism Professor of theology at Zurich 1924–1953 Influenced by Karl Barth, Søren Kierkegaard, and Jewish theologian Martin Buber.
HERMAN DOOYEWEERD	1894–1977	Netherlands	*A New Critique of Theoretical Thought* *In the Twilight of Western Thought*	Professor at the Free University of Amsterdam 1926–1967 Attempted to develop Christian political philosophy. Emphasized concept of "sphere sovereignty."

Chart 85

Prominent Protestant Missionaries

NAME	DATES	AREAS OF MINISTRY	HOME COUNTRY	CHURCH AFFILIATION	MISSION ORGANIZATION
JOHN ELIOT	1604–1690	North American Indians	England	Congregational	Society for the Propagation of the Gospel in New England
THOMAS BRAY	1656–1730	British North America	England	Anglican	Society for Promoting Christian Knowledge (founder) Society for the Propagation of the Gospel in Foreign Parts (founder)
BARTHOLOMAUS ZIEGENBALG	1684–1719	India	Germany	Lutheran	Danish-Halle Mission
DAVID BRAINERD	1718–1747	North American Indians	Connecticut Colony	Congregational	Scotch Society for Propagating Christian Knowledge
CHRISTIAN FRIEDRICH SCHWARTZ	1726–1798	India	Germany	Lutheran	Danish-Halle Mission
WILLIAM CAREY	1761–1834	India	England	Baptist	Baptist Missionary Society (founder)
HENRY MARTYN	1781–1812	India Persia	England	Anglican	British East India Company (chaplain)
ROBERT MORRISON	1782–1834	China	England	Anglican	London Missionary Society
ADONIRAM JUDSON	1788–1850	Burma	United States	Baptist	American Board of Commissioners for Foreign Missions (founder)
ROBERT MOFFAT	1795–1883	South Africa	Scotland	Wesleyan	London Missionary Society
ELIJAH C. BRIDGMAN	1801–1861	China	United States	Congregational	American Board of Commissioners for Foreign Missions
ALEXANDER DUFF	1806–1878	India	Scotland	Presbyterian	Church of Scotland
SAMUEL A. CROWTHER	c.1806–1891	Nigeria	Nigeria	Anglican	Church Missionary Society
JOHANN KRAPF	1810–1881	East Africa	Germany	Lutheran	Church Missionary Society

Chart 86

NAME	DATES	AREAS OF MINISTRY	HOME COUNTRY	CHURCH AFFILIATION	MISSION ORGANIZATION
DAVID LIVINGSTONE	1813–1873	Africa	Scotland	Independent	London Missionary Society
WILLIAM C. BURNS	1815–1868	China	Scotland	Presbyterian	English Presbyterian Church
JOHANNES REBMANN	1819–1876	East Africa	Germany	Lutheran	Church Missionary Society
JOHN G. PATON	1824–1907	New Hebrides	Scotland	Reformed Presbyterian	Reformed Presbyterian Church of Scotland
JOHN L. NEVIUS	1829–1893	China	United States	Presbyterian	Presbyterian Board of Foreign Missions
J. HUDSON TAYLOR	1832–1905	China	England	Wesleyan	China Inland Mission (founder)
H. GRATTAN GUINNESS	1835–1910	Congo	Ireland	Church of Ireland	Livingstone Inland Mission (founder) North Africa Mission (founder) Regions Beyond Missionary Union (founder)
MARY SLESSOR	1848–1915	West Africa	Scotland	Presbyterian	United Presbyterian Church of Scotland
JONATHAN GOFORTH	1859–1936	China	Canada	Presbyterian	Presbyterian Church of Canada
C. T. STUDD	1862–1931	China India Congo	England	Anglican	China Inland Mission Heart of Africa Mission (founder)
JOHN R. MOTT	1865–1955		United States	Methodist	Student Volunteer Movement World Student Christian Federation (founder)
AMY CARMICHAEL	1867–1951	Japan India	England	Anglican	Church of England Zenana Missionary Fellowship Dohnavur Fellowship (founder)
ALBERT SCHWEITZER	1875–1965	French Equatorial Africa	Germany	Lutheran	Paris Society of Evangelical Missions
E. STANLEY JONES	1884–1973	India	United States	Methodist	Methodist Church
L. NELSON BELL	1894–1973	China	United States	Southern Presbyterian	Southern Presbyterian Foreign Mission Society
JIM ELLIOT	1927–1956	Ecuador	United States	Presbyterian	Wycliffe Bible Translators

Chart 86

Prominent Roman Catholic Missionaries

NAME	DATES	AREAS OF MINISTRY	HOME COUNTRY	MONASTIC ORDER
BARTOLOMÉ DE LAS CASAS	1474–1566	Spanish America	Spain	Dominicans
FRANCIS XAVIER	1506–1552	India Ceylon East Indies Japan	Spain	Jesuits
FRANCIS SOLANUS	1549–1610	Spanish America	Spain	Franciscans
MATTEO RICCI	1552–1610	China	Italy	Jesuits
ROBERT DE NOBILI	1577–1656	India	Italy	Jesuits
ALEXANDER DE RHODES	b.1591	Vietnam	France	Jesuits
JOHANN ADAM SCHALL VON BELL	1591–1666	China	Germany	Jesuits
GUGLIELMO MASSAJA	1809–1889	Ethiopia	Italy	Capuchins
THEOPHILE VERBIST	1823–1868	Mongolia	Belgium	Scheutveld Fathers (founder)
CHARLES M. A. LAVIGERIE	1825–1892	North Africa	France	White Fathers (founder)
JOSEPH DAMIEN DE VEUSTER	1840–1889	Hawaii	Belgium	Picpus Fathers
CHARLES EUGENE DE FOUCAULD	1858–1916	North Africa	France	Trappists

Chart 87

Major Indigenous Christian Religious Movements in Africa

NAME OF MOVEMENT	NAME OF LEADER	CHURCH AFFILIATION	DATE OF ORIGIN	GEOGRAPHICAL AREA	DISTINCTIVES
THEMBU CHURCH	Nehemiah Tile	Methodist	1834	South Africa	Emphasized Thembu nationalism Wanted Thembu parliament to govern church on model of Church of England
ETHIOPIAN CHURCH	Mangena M. Mokone	Wesleyan	1892	South Africa	Opposition to European control in African church
ZIONIST APOSTOLIC CHURCH	Daniel Nkonyane	Dutch Reformed	1908	South Africa	Faith healing River baptism by immersion Speaking in tongues Polygamy Witchcraft real, but Satanic
AMA-SIRAYELI (Israelites)	Enoch Mgijima	Anglican	1910	South Africa	Halley's Comet a sign to the church Rejection of New Testament, return to Old Testament roots Faith healing
HARRIS CHRISTIANS	William Wadé Harris	Methodist	1913	Ivory Coast Liberia Gold Coast	Faith healing Destruction of fetishes
	Malaki Musajakawi	Anglican	1913	Uganda	Rejection of doctors and medicine Encouragement of polygamy
MALAKITES	Garrick Sokari Braid	Anglican	c.1916	Nigeria	Self-designation: Second Elijah Supernatural visions Faith healing Rejection of doctors and medicine Prohibition of alcoholic beverages
KIMBANGUIST CHURCH	Simon Kimbangu	Baptist	1921	Congo	Faith healing Destruction of fetishes Rejection of polygamy
ALADURA CHURCHES	Joseph Sadare Sophia Odunlami David Odubanjo	Anglican	1920s	Nigeria	Prayer for healing and children Opposition to witchcraft as Satanic Visions and prophetic revelation

Chart 88

Modern Roman Catholic Ecumenical Councils

	COUNCIL OF TRENT	FIRST VATICAN COUNCIL	SECOND VATICAN COUNCIL
DATES	1545–1563	1869–1870	1962–1965
CALLED BY	Paul III	Pius IX	John XXIII
PAPAL BULL	Laetare Hierusalem	Aeterni Patris	Humanae Salutis
NUMBER AND DATES OF SESSIONS	3 sessions – 1545–1547, 1551–1552, 1562–1563	1 session – 12/8/69–7/18/70	4 sessions – 10/11–12/8/62; 9/29–12/4/63; 9/14–11/21/64; 9/14–12/8/65
KEY FIGURES	Paul III Julius III Pius IV James Laynez Giovanni Morone	Pius IX Henry Manning Karl J. Hefele Felix Dupanloup	John XXIII Paul VI Karl Rahner Hans Küng
CENTRAL FOCUS	Reform the church Halt Protestant Reformation	Papal infallibility	*Aggiornamento* – Updating the church
MAJOR DECISIONS	Tradition bears same authority as Scripture. Apocrypha was included in canon of Scripture. Vulgate was declared official Bible of the church. Protestant teachings on original sin and justification by faith alone were rejected. Number of sacraments were fixed at seven, giving grace *ex opere operato*. Transubstantiation was affirmed. Moral standards for clergy were reaffirmed. Index was greatly expanded by the addition of Protestant writings.	Promulgated dogma of papal infallibility when speaking *ex cathedra* on matters of faith and morals.	Protestants were referred to as "separated brethren." Dialogue with other faiths was encouraged. Translation and reading of Bible were encouraged. Mass was required to be in vernacular, with laity participating. Religious freedom for all was upheld. Excommunications of Great Schism of 1054 were revoked. Index was eliminated. Papal infallibility, tradition, Catholic Church as only way of salvation were reaffirmed. Veneration of Mary was encouraged. Laity were recognized as spiritual priests. Collegiality of pope and bishops was recognized.

Chart 89

Forerunners of Pentecostalism

GROUP	PERIOD	PLACE	KEY FIGURES	DISTINCTIVES
MONTANISTS	2nd–3rd centuries	Asia Minor	Montanus Priscilla Maximilla Tertullian	Believed and practiced continuing gift of prophecy and glossolalia. Emphasized strict moral purity. Expected imminent establishment of Kingdom of God with coming of the Age of the Holy Spirit.
CATHARI	11th–14th centuries	Europe	Raymund of Toulouse	Also known as Bogomils and Albigensians. Similar to ancient Manichaean heresy—dualistic, docetic. Rejected sex and marriage, Catholic sacraments, practicing only *consolamentum*. Practice of glossolalia connects them with Pentecostalism.
CAMISARDS	Late 17th century	Southern France	Pierre Jurieu	Engaged in violent revolt against Louis XIV after revocation of Edict of Nantes. Practiced gift of prophecy and glossolalia.
CATHOLIC APOSTOLIC CHURCH	Early 19th century	England	Edward Irving	Church practiced speaking in tongues, healings, prophecies. Believed apostolic gifts would accompany restoration of true apostolic office.
SECOND GREAT AWAKENING	Early 19th century	United States	Charles G. Finney Asa Mahan	Camp meetings included displays of glossolalia and extraordinary manifestations of the Spirit. "Oberlin Theology" emphasized perfectionism, believing that both man and society were capable of achieving perfection.
HOLINESS MOVEMENT	Mid to late 19th century	United States	B. T. Roberts Phoebe Palmer A. B. Simpson	Attempted to return to original distinctives of Methodism such as perfectionism and entire sanctification through a "second blessing."
KESWICK MOVEMENT	Late 19th century	England	T. D. Harford-Battersby Andrew Murray	Emphasized victorious living, sanctification through filling of the Holy Spirit.

Chart 90

The Growth and Development of the World Council of Churches

INTERNATIONAL MISSIONARY COUNCIL	FAITH AND ORDER	LIFE AND WORK
1910 – World Missionary Conference, Edinburgh, Scotland: "The Evangelization of the World in This Generation"		
1921 – International Missionary Council formed at Lake Mohonk, New York, USA		
1928 – International Missionary Council, Jerusalem, Palestine	1927 – Faith and Order, Lausanne, Switzerland	1925 – Life and Work, Stockholm, Sweden
1938 – International Missionary Council, Madras, India	1937 – Faith and Order, Edinburgh, Scotland	1937 – Life and Work, Oxford, England
	1938 Joint Committee, Utrecht, Netherlands	
1947 – International Missionary Council, Whitby, Canada	1948—World Council of Churches, Amsterdam, Netherlands: "Man's Disorder and God's Design"	
1952 – International Missionary Council, Willingen, Netherlands: "The Missionary Obligation of the Church"	1952 – Commission on Faith and Order, Lund, Sweden	
1958 – International Missionary Council, Ghana	1954—World Council of Churches, Evanston, Illinois, U.S.A.: "Christ, the Hope of the World"	
1961—International Missionary Council joins World Council of Churches, New Delhi, India: "Jesus Christ, the Light of the World"		
1963 – Commission on World Mission and Evangelism, Mexico City, Mexico: "Witness in Six Continents"	1963 – Commission on Faith and Order, Montreal, Canada	1968 – Department of Church and Society, Geneva, Switzerland: "Christians in the Technical and Social Revolutions of Our Time"
1968—World Council of Churches, Uppsala, Sweden: "Behold, I Make All Things New"		
1972 – World Council on World Missions and Evangelism, Bangkok, Thailand: "Salvation Today"	1971 – Commission on Faith and Order, Louvain, Belgium	
	1974 – Commission on Faith and Order, Accra, Ghana	
1975—World Council of Churches, Nairobi, Kenya		
	1978 – Commission on Faith and Order, Bangalore, India	1979 – Department of Church and Society, Cambridge, Massachusetts, USA
	1982 – Commission on Faith and Order, Budapest, Hungary	
1983—World Council of Churches, Vancouver, Canada—"Jesus Christ, The Life of the World"		
1983 – Commission on World Missions and Evangelism, Melbourne, Australia	1985 – Commission on Faith and Order, Stavanger, Norway	
1989 – Commission on World Missions and Evangelism, San Antonio, Texas, USA	1989 – Commission on Faith and Order, Budapest, Hungary	
1991—World Council of Churches, Camberra, Australia		
1996 – Commission on World Missions and Evangelism, Salvador, Brazil	1993 – Commission on Faith and Order, Santiago de Compostela, Spain	
1998—World Council of Churches, Harare, Zimbabwe		

Chart 91

Translations of the Bible into English

TRANSLATION	DATE	TRANSLATORS	COMMENTS
WYCLIFFE BIBLE	1380–1384	John Wycliffe and associates	Based on Latin Vulgate
TYNDALE BIBLE	1525–1530	William Tyndale	NT and Pentateuch; based on original language manuscript
COVERDALE BIBLE	1535	Miles Coverdale	Completion of Tyndale's work
MATTHEW'S BIBLE	1537	John Rogers	Used work of Tyndale and Coverdale
GREAT BIBLE	1539	Miles Coverdale	Revision of Matthew's Bible commissioned by Henry VIII
GENEVA BIBLE	1560	English Puritans in Geneva	Revision of Great Bible with Calvinistic notes
BISHOPS' BIBLE	1568	Matthew Parker and others	Revision of Great Bible; reaction against Puritanism of Geneva Bible
RHEIMS-DOUAI VERSION	1582 – NT 1610 – OT	Gregory Martin and other English Catholic scholars	Roman Catholic, based on Latin Vulgate, produced by English College in Rheims and later Douai
AUTHORIZED VERSION (King James Version)	1604–1611	54 English scholars of varying theological convictions	Commissioned by James I after Hampton Court Conference of 1604; elevated prose designed for oral reading; based on Textus Receptus
CHALLONER VERSION	1749–1750	Richard Challoner	Roman Catholic revision of Rheims-Douai Version; language similar to that of KJV
ALFORD TRANSLATION	1861 – NT 1869 – OT	Henry Alford	Produced by dean of Canterbury Cathedral
YOUNG'S LITERAL TRANSLATION	1862	Robert Young	Accurate but difficult-to-read translation by the author of Young's Analytical Concordance
DARBY TRANSLATION	1871	John Nelson Darby	Translation by early Plymouth Brethren leader and originator of dispensationalism
ENGLISH REVISED VERSION	1881–1885	65 English scholars of varying theological convictions	Used textual principles of Westcott and Hort; very literal
AMERICAN STANDARD VERSION	1901	American scholars working concurrently with English translators of Revised Version	Slight modification of English Revised Version, reflecting preferences of American scholars
THE NEW TESTAMENT IN MODERN SPEECH	1903	Richard F. Weymouth	Translation by a scholar of classical Greek
A NEW TRANSLATION OF THE BIBLE	1913 – NT 1924 – OT	James Moffatt	Free translation, not always faithful to text, very popular in Britain
THE COMPLETE BIBLE: An American Translation	1923 – NT 1927 – OT	J. M. P. Smith E. J. Goodspeed	Highly readable translation by two American scholars

Chart 92

Translations of the Bible into English (continued)

TRANSLATION	DATE	TRANSLATORS	COMMENTS
CONFRATERNITY VERSION	1941	Edward P. Arbez and other Catholic scholars	Revision of Challoner Version; translated from Latin Vulgate
KNOX VERSION	1944 – NT 1949 – OT	Ronald Knox	Roman Catholic, based on Vulgate
REVISED STANDARD VERSION	1946 – NT 1952 – OT	32 American scholars, largely ecumenical in outlook	Sponsored by National Council of Churches; revision of the American Standard Version
THE NEW TESTAMENT: A New Translation in Plain English	1952	C. K. Williams	Emphasizes simplicity of vocabulary
THE AUTHENTIC NEW TESTAMENT	1955	Hugh Schonfield	Attempt to bring out the Jewish context of New Testament, translated by Jewish author of *The Passover Plot*
NEW WORLD TRANSLATION OF THE HOLY SCRIPTURES	1955 (revised 1961, 1970, 1984)	Nathan H. Knorr, Frederick W. Franz, and others	Jehovah's Witnesses translation, emphasizing their theological distinctives
THE NEW TESTAMENT IN MODERN ENGLISH	1958 (revised 1972)	J. B. Phillips	Free translation, lively language
BERKELEY VERSION	1945 – NT 1959 – OT	Gerrit Verkuyl (NT) 20 conservative scholars (OT)	Compiled in Berkeley, CA; also known as Modern Language Bible
AMPLIFIED BIBLE	1958 – NT 1965 – OT	12 editors	Produced in California; a smorgasbord of variant wordings
JERUSALEM BIBLE	1966	Roman Catholic School of Biblical Studies in Jerusalem	First Catholic Bible in English to rely extensively on original-language manuscripts
BARCLAY NEW TESTAMENT	1969	William Barclay	Translation by popular British preacher and writer
NEW ENGLISH BIBLE	1961 – NT 1970 – OT	C. H. Dodd and other British scholars of varying theological convictions	Sponsored by churches and Bible societies in Great Britain; makes extensive use of textual emendations
NEW AMERICAN BIBLE	1970	Catholic scholars of the Episcopal Confraternity of Christian Doctrine	Revision of 1941 Confraternity Version, more formal than Jerusalem Bible
NEW AMERICAN STANDARD BIBLE	1963 – NT 1971 – OT	Evangelical scholars	Revision of American Standard Version; sponsored by Lockman Foundation; most literal of mid 20th century translations
LIVING BIBLE	1971	Kenneth Taylor	Loose but highly readable paraphrase
GOOD NEWS BIBLE (Today's English Version)	1966 – NT 1976 – OT	Robert Bratcher	Sponsored by American Bible Society; uses principle of "dynamic equivalence"; simplified vocabulary

Chart 92

Translations of the Bible into English (continued)

TRANSLATION	DATE	TRANSLATORS	COMMENTS
NEW INTERNATIONAL VERSION	1973 – NT 1978 – OT	Edwin Palmer and 115 other evangelical scholars	Sponsored by the New York Bible Society (now the International Bible Society); translators from many English-speaking countries; combines accuracy and readability
NEW KING JAMES VERSION	1982	Arthur L. Farstad and 130 other evangelical scholars	Sponsored by Thomas Nelson Publishers; update of KJV, using Textus Receptus
READER'S DIGEST BIBLE	1982	Bruce Metzger and others	Condensed to about 60% of original length; reflects critical scholarship in introductions
NEW JERUSALEM BIBLE	1985	Henry Wansbrough and other Catholic scholars	Revision of Jerusalem Bible seeking greater accuracy; uses some inclusive language
NEW CENTURY VERSION	1987	Ervin Bishop and others	Also known as International Children's Bible; originally intended for the deaf using simplified vocabulary; dynamic equivalence translation
NEW REVISED STANDARD VERSION	1990	Bruce Metzger and others	Modernized language of RSV; thoroughly gender inclusive; even more liberal than original in Old Testament
CONTEMPORARY ENGLISH VERSION	1991 – NT 1995 – OT	Barclay Newman and others	Paraphrase set at fourth-grade reading level; omits theological concepts and terms; strongly gender-neutral
NEW LIVING TRANSLATION	1996	Mark Norton and 90 evangelical scholars	Paraphrase, but not as loose as the original Living Bible; uses dynamic equivalence; gender-neutral language
NET BIBLE (New English Translation)	1998 – NT 2000 – OT	W. Hall Harris and about 20 other evangelical scholars	Designed to be posted free on the Internet; constantly revised based on input from readers; involved significant input from staffers at Summer Institute of Linguistics
HOLMAN CHRISTIAN STANDARD BIBLE	2001	Edwin Blum and other evangelical scholars	Sponsored by Broadman and Holman, Southern Baptist publishing house; avoids gender-neutral language
ENGLISH STANDARD VERSION	2001	J. I. Packer, Wayne Grudem, and other evangelical scholars	Evangelical reworking of the Revised Standard Version; avoids gender-neutral language; seeks accuracy of New American Standard Bible and readability of New International Version
THE MESSAGE: The Bible in Contemporary Language	1993–NT 2002–OT	Eugene Peterson	Vivid language, but looser than most paraphrases, with many insertions and omissions
TODAY'S NEW INTERNATIONAL VERSION	2002 – NT 2005 – OT	International Bible Society	Gender-neutral revision of the NIV

Chart 92

Notable Protestant Historians of the Church

NAME	DATES	BIRTHPLACE	CHURCH AFFILIATION	PERIOD CHRONICLED	REPRESENTATIVE HISTORICAL WORKS
JOHN FOXE	1516–1587	Lincolnshire, England	Anglican	Early church to 1556, concentrating on Marian persecution in England	*The Acts and Monuments of the Church* (*Foxe's Book of Martyrs*)
MATTHIAS FLACIUS ILLYRICUS	1520–1575	Illyria	Lutheran	Complete to Reformation	*The Magdeburg Centuries* (editor) — 13 vols.
COTTON MATHER	1663–1728	Boston, MA	Congregational	17th century Puritan New England	*Magnalia Christi Americana*
J. A. W. NEANDER	1789–1850	Göttingen, Germany	Lutheran	Complete	*General History of the Christian Religion and Church*—6 vols.
J. H. MERLE D'AUBIGNÉ	1794–1872	Geneva, Switzerland	Evangelical Church of Switzerland	Reformation	*History of the Reformation of the Sixteenth Century*—5 vols. *History of the Reformation in Europe at the Time of Calvin*—8 vols. *History of the Reformation in England*—2 vols.
WILLIAM CUNNINGHAM	1805–1861	Hamilton, Scotland	Free Church of Scotland	History of Theology	*Historical Theology* *The Reformers and the Theology of the Reformation*
PHILIP SCHAFF	1819–1893	Chur, Switzerland	German Reformed	Apostolic Age through Reformation	*History of the Christian Church*—8 vols. *The Creeds of Christendom*—3 vols.
ADOLF VON HARNACK	1851–1930	Dorpat, Estonia	Lutheran	Ante-Nicene period	*History of Dogma* *The Mission and Expansion of Christianity in the First Three Centuries*

Chart 93

NAME	DATES	BIRTHPLACE	CHURCH AFFILIATION	PERIOD CHRONICLED	REPRESENTATIVE HISTORICAL WORKS
WILLISTON WALKER	1860–1922	Portland, ME	Congregational	Complete	*History of the Christian Church* *A History of the Congregational Churches in the United States* *The Reformation*
WILLIAM W. SWEET	1881–1959	Baldwin, KS	Methodist	American Church History	*The Story of Religion in America* *Religion on the American Frontier* *Methodism in American History*
KENNETH SCOTT LATOURETTE	1884–1968	Oregon	Baptist	Complete	*A History of Christianity* *History of the Expansion of Christianity—7 vols.* *Christianity in a Revolutionary Age—5 vols.*
SYDNEY AHLSTROM	1919–1984	Cokato, MN	Lutheran	American Church History	*Theology in America* *A Religious History of the American People—2 vols.*
MARTIN E. MARTY	b.1928	West Point, NE	Lutheran	American Church History	*Modern American Religion—3 vols.* *Righteous Empire* *The One and the Many: America's Search for the Common Good*

Chart 93

THE
AMERICAN CHURCH
(FROM 1607)

A Timeline of the Church in the American Colonies (1607–1776)

	1580 AD–1600 AD	1600 AD–1620 AD	1620 AD–1640 AD	1640 AD–1660 AD	1660 AD–1680 AD
PEOPLE	John Cotton (1584–1652) Thomas Hooker (1586–1647) Anne Hutchinson (1591–1643) Richard Mather (1596–1669)	Roger Williams (c.1603–c.1683) John Eliot (1604–1690) Thomas Shepherd (1605–1649) Cecil Calvert, Lord Baltimore (1605–1675) John Harvard (1607–1638)	Increase Mather (1639–1723)	Solomon Stoddard (1643–1729) William Penn (1644–1718) Francis Makemie (1658–1708)	Cotton Mather (1663–1728) William Tennent (1673–1746) Experience Mayhew (1673–1758)
EVENTS		Jamestown settlement (1607) Pilgrims land at Plymouth (1620)	Massachusetts Bay Colony (1629) Lord Baltimore establishes Maryland (1634) Harvard College (1636)	Roger Williams founds Rhode Island (1644) Cambridge Platform (1648)	Half-Way Covenant (1662) British seize New York from Dutch (1664)

Chart 94

A Timeline of the Church in the American Colonies (1607–1776), continued

	1680 AD–1700 AD	1700 AD–1720 AD	1720 AD–1740 AD	1740 AD–1760 AD	1760 AD–1780 AD
PEOPLE	Theodore J. Frelinghuysen (1691–c.1748) Jonathan Dickenson (1698–1747)	Jonathan Edwards (1703–1758) Gilbert Tennent (1703–1764) Charles Chauncy (1705–1787) Shubal Stearns (1706–1771) Daniel Marshall (1706–1784) Eleazar Wheelock (1711–1779) Henry Melchior Muhlenberg (1711–1787) Samuel Blair (1712–1751) George Whitefield (1714–1770) James Davenport (1716–1757) David Brainerd (1718–1747)	Jonathan Mayhew (1720–1766) Samuel Hopkins (1721–1803) David Zeisberger (1721–1808) Samuel Davies (1723–1761) John Witherspoon (1723–1794) Devereux Jarratt (1723–1801) Isaac Backus (1724–1806)	Francis Asbury (1745–1816) Thomas Coke (1747–1814)	
EVENTS	William Penn founds Pennsylvania (1681) Salem Witch Trials (1692) College of William and Mary (1693)	Yale College (1701)	First Great Awakening (c.1725–c.1760) James Oglethorpe founds Georgia (1732) Wesleys arrive in Georgia (1735) Log College (1735)	Old Side/New Side schism (1741–1758) College of New Jersey (1746)	Queens College (1764) American Revolution (1776–1783)

Chart 94

A Timeline of the Church in the United States (from 1776)

	1760 AD–1780 AD	1780 AD–1800 AD	1800 AD–1820 AD	1820 AD–1840 AD	1840 AD–1860 AD
PEOPLE	Timothy Dwight (1752–1817) James McGready (c.1758–1817) Richard Allen (1760–1831) Thomas Campbell (1763–1854) Barton Stone (1772–1844) Archibald Alexander (1772–1851) Lyman Beecher (1775–1863) William Ellery Channing (1780–1842)	William Miller (1782–1849) Asahel Nettleton (1783–1844) Peter Cartwright (1785–1872) Nathaniel Taylor (1786–1858) Adoniram Judson (1788–1850) Alexander Campbell (1788–1866) Charles G. Finney (1792–1875) Charles Hodge (1797–1878)	John Nelson Darby (1800–1882) Brigham Young (1801–1877) Theodore Weld (1803–1895) Joseph Smith (1805–1844) Harriet Beecher Stowe (1811–1896) Robert L. Dabney (1820–1898)	Mary Baker Eddy (1821–1910) Ellen G. White (1827–1915) Dwight L. Moody (1837–1899) Frances Willard (1839–1898)	Charles A. Briggs (1841–1913) William E. Blackstone (1841–1935) C. I. Scofield (1843–1921) Benjamin B. Warfield (1851–1921) Charles Taze Russell (1852–1916) Reuben A. Torrey (1856–1928) J. Wilbur Chapman (1859–1918)
EVENTS			Camp meeting at Cane Ridge, KY (1801) Plan of Union (1801–1837) Haystack Prayer Meeting (1806) Princeton Theological Seminary (1812) American Colonization Society (1817)		

Chart 95

A Timeline of the Church in the United States (from 1776), continued

	1860 AD–1880 AD	1880 AD–1900 AD	1900 AD–1920 AD	1920 AD–1940 AD	1940 AD–1960 AD
PEOPLE	Walter Rauschenbusch (1861–1918) Charles H. Brent (1862–1929) Billy Sunday (1862–1935) John R. Mott (1865–1955) Lewis Sperry Chafer (1871–1952) Charles F. Parham (1873–1929) Louis Berkhof (1873–1957) Harry Emerson Fosdick (1878–1969)	J. Gresham Machen (1881–1937) Kenneth Scott Latourette (1884–1968) Reinhold Niebuhr (1892–1971) J. Oliver Buswell (1895–1977) Cornelius Van Til (1895–1987) John Murray (1898–1975)	Carl McIntire (1906–2002) John F. Walvoord (1910–2002) Francis Schaeffer (1912–1985) Carl F. H. Henry (1913–2003) Billy Graham (b.1918) Sydney Ahlstrom (1919–1984)	Martin Marty (b.1928) Martin Luther King (1929–1968) Alvin Plantinga (b.1932) Jerry Falwell (b.1933) James Dobson (b.1936) James M. Boice (1938–2000)	
EVENTS	Civil War (1861–1865) Women's Christian Temperance Union (1874)		Federal Council of Churches (1908) *The Fundamentals* (1910–1915) Prohibition Amendment (1919–1932)	Auburn Affirmation (1924) Dallas Theological Seminary (1924) Scopes Trial (1925) Westminster Theological Seminary (1929)	National Association of Evangelicals (1942) National Council of Churches (1950)

Chart 95

Religion in the Thirteen Colonies

COLONY	CHARTER DATE	CHARTER RECIPIENT	FIRST SETTLED	SETTLED BY	MAIN REASON FOR COMING	RELIGIOUS ORIENTATION	ESTABLISHED CHURCH
VIRGINIA	1606	Virginia Company	1607	English	Economic gain	Anglican	Church of England
	1624	Royal Colony					
MASSACHUSETTS	1619	Pilgrims	1620	Pilgrims	Religious freedom	Separatist	Congregationalist
	1629	Massachusetts Bay Company		Puritans	Establish theocracy	Congregationalist	
	1684	Royal Colony					
NEW HAMPSHIRE	1679	Royal Colony	1623	Puritan	Expansion from Massachusetts Bay	Congregationalist	Congregationalist
NEW YORK	1664	Royal Colony	1624	Dutch	Economic gain	Dutch Reformed	Church of England (1692)
MARYLAND	1632	Lord Baltimore	1634	English	Refuge for Roman Catholics Personal empire for Calverts	Roman Catholics and others	Church of England (1691)
	1691	Royal Colony					
CONNECTICUT	1662	John Winthrop Jr. (Royal Colony)	1634	Puritans	Expansion from Massachusetts Bay	Congregationalist	Congregationalist
RHODE ISLAND	1644	Roger Williams	1636	English	Radicals fleeing Massachusetts Bay	Congregationalist	None
	1663	Renewed					
NEW JERSEY	1664	John Berkeley, George Carteret	1638	Swedish	Economic gain	Lutheran	None
	1702	Royal Colony		Dutch	Expansion from New York	Dutch Reformed	
	1683	Duke of York		English	Religious freedom	Quaker	
DELAWARE			1638	Swedish		Lutheran	None
	1693	Part of Pennsylvania		Dutch	Economic gain	Dutch Reformed	
	1704	Separate government		English		Anglican	
NORTH CAROLINA	1712	Separate government from SC	1653	English	Economic gain	Anglican	Church of England
	1729	Royal Colony					
SOUTH CAROLINA	1663	Carolina Company	1670	English	Economic gain	Anglican	Church of England (1704)
				French	Religious freedom	Huguenots	
PENNSYLVANIA	1681	William Penn	1681	English	Religious freedom	Quaker	None
				German	Fleeing Thirty Years' War	Lutheran	
				German	Religious Freedom	Mennonite, Brethren, Amish, Schwenkfelder, Moravian	
GEORGIA	1732	James Oglethorpe	1733	English	Relief for those in debtors' prison	Anglican	Church of England (1758)
	1752	Royal Colony		German	Religious freedom	Moravian	

Chart 96

Religious Utopian Communities in America

GROUP	LEADERS	LOCATION	DISTINCTIVES
ORDER OF THE SOLITARY (Ephrata Cloister)	Conrad Beissel (1690–1768) John Peter Miller (1710–1796)	Ephrata, PA	Strict asceticism Seventh-day Sabbath Pacifism Communalism Believers' baptism
UNITED SOCIETY OF BELIEVERS IN CHRIST'S SECOND APPEARING (Shakers)	Ann Lee Stanley (1736–1784) Joseph Meacham (1741–1796)	New Lebanon, NY Union Village, OH 17 other communities in New England and Midwest	Mother Ann Lee's belief that she was Christ in his second coming Sexual relations the root of all evil Pacifism Universalism Communication with dead Speaking in tongues Group dancing (source of common name) Auricular confession Communalism God both male and female Millennium began in 1787
THE SOCIETY OF THE PUBLIC UNIVERSAL FRIEND	Jemima Wilkinson (1752–1819)	Lake Seneca, NY Crooked Lake, NY	Jemima Wilkinson's becoming the Public Universal Friend, the Publisher of Truth, after dying and having her body inhabited by the Spirit of Life. Wilkinson believed to be Christ in his second coming by her followers. Celibacy
HARMONY SOCIETY (Rappites)	George Rapp (1757–1847)	Harmony, PA New Harmony, IN Economy, OH	Universalism Celibacy Auricular confession Communalism Uniform dress Rejection of sacraments Opposition to education
COMMUNITY OF TRUE INSPIRATION (Amana Church Society)	Michael Krausert Christian Metz Barbara Heinemann (1795–1883)	Ebenezer, NY Amana, IA	Influenced by German Pietism Communalism Pacifism Leaders divinely inspired Now a corporation
ONEIDA COMMUNITY	John Humphrey Noyes (1811–1886)	Oneida, NY Wallingford, CT	Perfectionism Communal "complex marriage" Procreation by communal decision on eugenic basis Communalism Manufacture of traps and silverware

Chart 97

The American Puritans

NAME	DATES	EDUCATION	REPRESENTATIVE WRITINGS	NOTABLE FACTS
JOHN COTTON	1584–1652	Cambridge	*The Keys of the Kingdom of Heaven* *The Way of the Churches of Christ in New England*	Was Anglican pastor 1612–1633. Forced from England by Archbishop Laud. Served as pastor of First Congregational Church in Boston for almost 20 years. Advocated exile of Roger Williams and Anne Hutchinson.
THOMAS HOOKER	1586–1647	Cambridge		Left England because of persecution by Archbishop Laud. Spent three years in the Netherlands. Accompanied Cotton to Massachusetts Bay in 1633. Moved congregation to Connecticut, founded Hartford. Helped write constitution for Connecticut colony.
RICHARD MATHER	1596–1669	Oxford	*Bay Psalm Book*	Was suspended from ministry by Archbishop Laud in 1633. Served as pastor at Dorchester, MA, from 1636. Advocated Half-Way Covenant (1662).
ROGER WILLIAMS	c.1603–c.1683	Cambridge		Was ordained in Anglican church, later moved toward Separatism. Came to New England in 1631, seeking liberty of conscience. Conflicts forced moves from Boston to Plymouth to Salem. Was expelled from Massachusetts Bay in 1635. Founded Providence, Rhode Island. Started first Baptist church in America in 1639.

Chart 98

NAME	DATES	EDUCATION	REPRESENTATIVE WRITINGS	NOTABLE FACTS
THOMAS SHEPHERD	1605–1649	Cambridge	*The Sincere Convert*	Fled to New England in 1635 to escape Archbishop Laud. Became pastor at Cambridge, MA. Defended American Puritans against accusations of cowardice and independency.
INCREASE MATHER	1639–1723	Harvard	*A Brief History of the Wars with the Indians* *An Essay for the Recording of Illustrious Providences*	Was son of Richard Mather. Served as pastor in England until Restoration. Was pastor of North Church, Boston, from 1664. Advocated Half-Way Covenant. Was president of Harvard 1684–1701.
SOLOMON STODDARD	1643–1729	Harvard	*A Guide to Christ* *A Treatise Concerning Conversion*	Became first librarian of Harvard College. Served as pastor at Northampton, MA, from 1670. Believed in regenerating power of Lord's Supper. Advocated Half-Way Covenant. Was grandfather of Jonathan Edwards.
COTTON MATHER	1663–1728	Harvard	*Magnalia Christi Americana* *Memorable Providences Relating to Witchcraft and Possessions*	Was son of Increase Mather. Graduated from Harvard at age 15. Assisted father at North Church in Boston. Opposed decline of Puritan theocracy. Spoke out against 1692 Salem witch trials. Was admitted to Royal Society in 1713.

Chart 98

Leaders of the First Great Awakening

NAME	DATES	COLONY	CHURCH AFFILIATION	NOTABLE FACTS
WILLIAM TENNENT	1673–1746	Pennsylvania	Presbyterian	Was born in Ireland. Came to Philadelphia in 1717. In 1735 built "Log College" to train ministers, many of whom participated in the First Great Awakening.
THEODORE J. FRELINGHUYSEN	1691–c.1748	New Jersey	Dutch Reformed	Was born in East Friesland. Came to Raritan River area in 1720. Alienated parishioners by refusing Communion to some of church's elders. Was instrumental in forming Dutch Reformed Church in America.
JONATHAN EDWARDS	1703–1758	Massachusetts	Congregational	Was grandson of Solomon Stoddard. Knew Hebrew, Greek, and Latin when he entered Yale at age 13. Became pastor in Northampton, MA, where God brought great revival. Served as missionary to Indians after being ejected from his church. Became president of the College of New Jersey (now Princeton) in 1758. Was possibly the greatest theologian America ever produced. Wrote *Religious Affections, The Freedom of the Will, Narrative of the Surprising Work of God.* Died of smallpox inoculation.
GILBERT TENNENT	1703–1764	Pennsylvania New Jersey	Presbyterian	Was eldest son of William Tennent. Was trained in Log College. Worked with Frelinghuysen. Traveled with Whitefield. Preached "Danger of an Unconverted Ministry." Helped start College of New Jersey (Princeton).
SHUBAL STEARNS	1706–1771	Southern colonies	Baptist	Was born in Boston. Became converted under Whitefield's preaching. In 1758 formed Baptist Association in Sandy Creek, NC.

Chart 99

NAME	DATES	COLONY	CHURCH AFFILIATION	NOTABLE FACTS
DANIEL MARSHALL	1706–1784	Southern colonies	Baptist	Was born in Windsor, CT. Spent two years as missionary to Indians. Was brother-in-law and associate of Stearns. Helped organize Georgia Baptist Association.
ELEAZAR WHEELOCK	1711–1779	Connecticut	Congregational	Graduated from Yale. Was associate of Jonathan Edwards. Was founder and first president of Dartmouth, founded to train Indians as missionaries.
HENRY MELCHIOR MUHLENBERG	1711–1787	Pennsylvania	Lutheran	Was called Father of American Lutheranism. Was born in Hanover, Germany. Graduated from University of Göttingen. Was influenced by Pietism at Halle. Came to Pennsylvania in 1742. Formed first Lutheran Synod in America.
SAMUEL BLAIR	1712–1751	Pennsylvania New Jersey	Presbyterian	Studied under William Tennent at Log College. Served as pastor in Pennsylvania and New Jersey. Was associate of Gilbert Tennent. Started school in Foggs Manor, PA.
GEORGE WHITEFIELD	1714–1770	Traveled throughout colonial America	Anglican	Was member of Holy Club at Oxford. Was early friend of the Wesleys. Became most famous evangelist of his day. Made seven trips to American colonies. Was catalyst of First Great Awakening. Knew Edwards, Frelinghuysen, Tennents. Befriended and admired by Benjamin Franklin.
SAMUEL DAVIES	1723–1761	Virginia	Presbyterian	Studied under Samuel Blair. In 1747 helped form presbytery in Hanover County, VA. Helped found and served as president of College of New Jersey (Princeton).

Chart 99

Religious Influences Supporting the American Revolution

GROUPS WHO SUPPORTED REVOLUTION

REASONS FOR SUPPORTING REVOLUTION	CONGREGA-TIONALISTS	PRESBYTERIANS	ANGLICAN LAYMEN (S. COLONIES)	LUTHERANS	RADICAL DISSENTERS
Covenantal view of society – A government that violates God's covenant forfeits its right to obedience.	✓	✓			
Religious freedom is possible only when there is political freedom.	✓	✓	✓	✓	✓
Deist emphasis on natural law and human rights.			✓		
Fear of Anglican establishment, renewed persecution.	✓	✓			✓
Fear of Anglican establishment, desire to see their own churches established.	✓	✓		✓	
Fear of Anglican establishment, desire to minimize religious interference in political affairs.			✓		
Fear of Anglican establishment, rejection of establishment as general principle.					✓

Chart 100

Religious Influences Opposed to the American Revolution

REASONS FOR OPPOSING REVOLUTION	GROUPS WHO OPPOSED REVOLUTION			
	ANGLICAN CLERGY	ANGLICAN LAYMEN (NEW ENGLAND AND MIDDLE COLONIES)	RADICAL DISSENTERS	METHODISTS
Biblical requirement to submit to rulers as ordained by God.	✓	✓		✓
Oath of loyalty to king sacred according to Scripture.	✓			
God's favor of order of British rule over the anarchy that may replace it.	✓	✓		
British rule seen as an aid to Anglican establishment.	✓	✓		
Influence of John Wesley's "Calm Address to the American Colonies."				✓
Support of pacifism as a general principle.			✓	

Chart 101

Leaders of the Second Great Awakening

NAME	DATES	BIRTHPLACE	CHURCH AFFILIATION	SCHOOLS FOUNDED AND/OR TAUGHT AT	NOTABLE FACTS
FRANCIS ASBURY	1745–1816	Birmingham, England	Methodist		In 1784 was appointed bishop for North America by John Wesley. Differed with Wesley over American Revolution. Pioneered circuit riding. Traveled about 300,000 miles on horseback. Methodist Church in U.S. grew by over 200,000 members under his leadership.
TIMOTHY DWIGHT	1752–1817	Northampton, MA	Congregational	Yale College (president 1795–1817)	Was grandson of Jonathan Edwards. While at Yale started revival that soon spread to other colleges. Became poet and hymn writer.
JAMES McGREADY	c.1758–1817	Western Pennsylvania	Presbyterian		Served as pastor in North Carolina, Kentucky. Originated camp meeting, July 1800. Helped found Cumberland Presbyterian Church.
THOMAS CAMPBELL	1763–1854	Scotland	Presbyterian	Bethany College (founder in 1840)	Came to America in 1807. Resigned from Presbyterian Church. Began independent ministry, which was taken over by his son; group became Disciples of Christ.
BARTON W. STONE	1772–1844	Port Tobacco, MD	Presbyterian		Was converted under McGready's preaching. Organized famous camp meeting in Cane Ridge, KY, in 1801. Founded Christian Church, which later merged with Disciples of Christ.
LYMAN BEECHER	1775–1863	New Haven, CT	Presbyterian	Lane Theological Seminary (president 1832–1852)	Was student of Dwight at Yale. Became successful pastor and evangelist. Was noted social reformer—opposed slavery, alcoholic beverages, dueling. Helped found American Bible Society. Was father of Henry Ward Beecher and Harriet Beecher Stowe.

Chart 102

NAME	DATES	BIRTHPLACE	CHURCH AFFILIATION	SCHOOLS FOUNDED AND/OR TAUGHT AT	NOTABLE FACTS
ASAHEL NETTLETON	1783–1844	North Killingworth, CT	Congregational	Theological Institute of Connecticut (helped to found in 1833, lectured there occasionally)	Was called to missionary work abroad, but poor health and success in revivals at home prevented it. Began evangelistic work in rural Connecticut. Poor health forced him into semi-retirement in 1820. Opposed New Haven Theology and Finney's New Measures.
BENNET TYLER	1783–1858	Connecticut	Congregational	Dartmouth College (president 1822–1828); Theological Institute of Connecticut (president 1833–1858)	Was student of Dwight at Yale. Served as pastor in Portland, ME. Opposed innovations in New Haven Theology. Wrote biography of Nettleton.
PETER CARTWRIGHT	1785–1872	Amherst County, VA	Methodist		Licensed as exhorter at age 17, later ordained by Francis Asbury. Carried on itinerant ministry in Kentucky and Tennessee, but left South in 1824 because of disillusionment with slavery. Continued preaching for next 48 years in Illinois. Served in Illinois State Legislature. Defeated by Abraham Lincoln in run for Congress in 1846.
NATHANIEL WILLIAM TAYLOR	1786–1858	New Milford, CT	Congregational	Yale Divinity School (taught 1822–1858)	Was student of Dwight at Yale. Served as pastor of First Church, New Haven, CT. Was major developer of New Haven Theology.
ALEXANDER CAMPBELL	1788–1866	Northern Ireland	Presbyterian	Bethany College (founder and president 1840–1866)	Was son of Thomas Campbell. Studied in Glasgow. Published periodicals *The Christian Baptist* and *The Millennial Harbinger*. Founded Disciples of Christ. Merged with followers of Barton Stone in 1832.
CHARLES G. FINNEY	1792–1875	Warren, CT	Presbyterian	Oberlin College (taught 1835–1866; president from 1851)	Was trained in law. Was converted in 1821, licensed shortly after. Originated New Measures in evangelism. Taught entire sanctification. Opposed by Beecher and Nettleton. Was an active abolitionist.

Chart 102

A Comparison of the First and Second Great Awakenings

	FIRST GREAT AWAKENING	SECOND GREAT AWAKENING
TIME FRAME	Early to mid 18th century	Early to mid 19th century
FORMATIVE ENVIRONMENT	Failure of Puritan theocracy	Frontier expansion
MAJOR FIGURES	Theodore J. Frelinghuysen William Tennent Gilbert Tennent Jonathan Edwards George Whitefield	Francis Asbury James McGready Barton Stone Peter Cartwright Charles G. Finney
MOST ACTIVE DENOMINATIONS	Dutch Reformed Presbyterian Congregational	Methodist Baptist
CHARACTERISTIC METHODS	Doctrinal preaching in churches	Circuit riding Camp meetings Revivals in churches
THEOLOGICAL ORIENTATION	Calvinist	Arminian
CHARACTERISTIC EMPHASIS	Doctrine	Experience
NEGATIVE SIDE EFFECTS	Unitarianism	American cults

Chart 103

Major Nineteenth-Century Evangelical Social Reform Movements

REFORM MOVEMENT	KEY EVANGELICAL LEADERS	REFORM ORGANIZATIONS	RESULTS ACHIEVED
ABOLITION OF SLAVERY	Samuel Hopkins (1721–1803) Lyman Beecher (1775–1863) Arthur Tappan (1786–1865) Charles G. Finney (1792–1875) John Brown (1800–1859) Theodore Weld (1803–1895) Jonathan Blanchard (1811–1892) Harriet Beecher Stowe (1811–1896)	1807 – Friends of Humanity Association 1817 – American Colonization Society 1818 – American Conventions for Promoting the Abolition of Slavery and Improving the Condition of the African Race 1833 – American Anti-Slavery Society 1840 – Liberty Party 1848 – Free Soil Party	1820 – Colonization of Liberia 1861–1865 – Civil War 1863 – Emancipation Proclamation 1865 – Thirteenth Amendment 1866 – Fourteenth Amendment
PROHIBITION OF ALCOHOLIC BEVERAGES	Lyman Beecher (1775–1863) Frances Willard (1839–1898) Carrie Nation (1846–1911) Billy Sunday (1862–1935)	1813 – Massachusetts Society for the Suppression of Intemperance 1826 – American Society for the Promotion of Temperance 1836 – American Temperance Union 1840 – Washingtonians 1869 – National Prohibition Party 1874 – Women's Christian Temperance Union 1893 – Anti-Saloon League	1846 – Maine passed Prohibition Ordinance 1847–1855 – Thirteen other states followed 1919–1932 – Prohibition Amendment in force
WOMEN'S RIGHTS	Emma Willard (1787–1870) Matthew Vassar (1792–1868) Angelina Grimke (1792–1873) Mary Lyon (1797–1849)	1848 – Women's Rights Convention 1869 – National Woman Suffrage Association 1869 – American Woman Suffrage Association 1892 – Federal Woman Suffrage Association	1821 – "Female Seminary" founded in Troy, NY 1836 – Mt. Holyoke College founded 1861 – Vassar College founded 1917 – Suffrage to women granted by New York 1918 – Fourteen other states followed 1920 – Woman Suffrage Amendment

Chart 104

Denominational Schisms over Slavery

DENOMINATION	YEAR OF DIVISION	NORTHERN ORGANIZATION	SOUTHERN ORGANIZATION	YEAR OF REUNION	NAME OF REUNITED CHURCH
METHODIST	1844	Methodist Episcopal Church	Methodist Episcopal Church, South	1939	United Methodist Church
BAPTIST	1845	American Baptist Missionary Union (now American Baptist Convention)	Southern Baptist Convention		
EPISCOPAL	1861	Protestant Episcopal Church	Protestant Episcopal Church in the Confederate States of America	1865	Protestant Episcopal Church
PRESBYTERIAN	1861	Presbyterian Church in the United States of America	Presbyterian Church in the Confederate States (later Presbyterian Church in the United States)	1983	United Presbyterian Church in the United States of America

Chart 105

Black Denominations in the United States

CHURCH	DATE OF FOUNDING	FOUNDERS	DISTINCTIVES
UNION AMERICAN METHODIST EPISCOPAL CHURCH	1813		Formed in Wilmington, DE. Exists almost exclusively on East Coast.
AFRICAN METHODIST EPISCOPAL CHURCH	1816	Richard Allen Absalom Jones	Began in Philadelphia with assistance of Francis Asbury. Largest black Methodist body in the United States.
AFRICAN METHODIST EPISCOPAL ZION CHURCH	1821	James Varick Peter Williams	Founded to protest discrimination in Methodist churches in New York.
SECOND CUMBERLAND PRESBYTERIAN CHURCH IN THE UNITED STATES	1869		Originally Colored Cumberland Presbyterian Church. Split from Cumberland Presbyterian Church, and shares its Second Awakening distinctives and departures from Calvinism.
CHRISTIAN METHODIST EPISCOPAL CHURCH	1870		Founded with assistance of Methodist Episcopal Church, South. Originally Colored Methodist Episcopal Church.
REFORMED METHODIST UNION EPISCOPAL CHURCH	1885		Split from African Methodist Episcopal Church. Shares episcopal organization of parent body. Practices love feasts in observance of Lord's Supper.
CHURCHES OF THE LIVING GOD	1889	William Christian	Based on the religious ideas of Freemasonry. Practices foot-washing, use water and unleavened bread in Communion.
CHURCH OF CHRIST (HOLINESS) USA	1894	C. P. Jones	Roots in Holiness Movement of Methodist Church. Practices foot-washing, divine healing.
NATIONAL BAPTIST CONVENTION, USA, INC.	1895	E. C. Morris	Largest black Baptist denomination in the United States. Operates seminary jointly with Southern Baptists. Has historically emphasized racial self-help.
CHURCH OF GOD AND SAINTS OF CHRIST	1896	William S. Crowdy	Celebrates Jewish feast days, observes seventh-day Sabbath. Combines black nationalism with "prophetic Judaism."

Chart 106

Black Denominations in the United States (continued)

CHURCH	DATE OF FOUNDING	FOUNDERS	DISTINCTIVES
NATIONAL PRIMITIVE BAPTIST CONVENTION OF THE USA	1907		Formerly Colored Primitive Baptist Church. Shares distinctives of other Primitive Baptists, including opposition to church organization.
NATIONAL BAPTIST CONVENTION OF AMERICA, INC.	1915	R. H. Boyd	Split from National Baptist Convention, USA over ownership of publishing house. Collaborates with National Baptist Convention, USA in missionary work.
APOSTOLIC OVERCOMING HOLY CHURCH OF GOD	1916	W. T. Phillips	Originally Ethiopian Overcoming Holy Church of God. Roots in Holiness Movement of Methodist Church. Stresses holiness, divine healing, avoidance of worldly practices.
AFRICAN ORTHODOX CHURCH	1921	George A. McGuire	Emphasizes apostolic succession. Observes seven sacraments of Roman Catholicism. Episcopal church government.
BIBLE WAY CHURCH, WORLDWIDE	1957		Split from Church of Our Lord of the Apostolic Faith. Shares Pentecostal emphases of parent body.
PROGRESSIVE NATIONAL BAPTIST CONVENTION, INC.	1961	Martin Luther King Jr. Ralph Abernathy Gardner C. Taylor	Split from National Baptist Convention, USA over involvement in Civil Rights Movement. Ecumenical in philosophy.
NATIONAL MISSIONARY BAPTIST CONVENTION OF AMERICA	1988		Split from National Baptist Convention of America over ownership of publishing house (wanted Convention control rather than that of Boyd family).

Chart 106

Major Nineteenth-Century American Cults

	MORMONS	ADVENTISTS		CHRISTIAN SCIENCE	JEHOVAH'S WITNESSES
OFFICIAL NAME	Church of Jesus Christ of Latter-Day Saints	Seventh-Day Adventists		Church of Christ, Scientist	Zion's Watchtower Bible and Tract Society
FOUNDER(S)	Joseph Smith Jr. (1805–1844)	William Miller (1782–1849) [movement]	Former followers of Miller [church]	Mary Baker Glover Patterson Eddy (1821–1910)	Charles Taze Russell (1852–1916)
DATE	1830	1844	1860	1879	1884
PLACE	Harmony, PA	Upstate NY	Battle Creek, MI	Boston, MA	Pittsburgh, PA
OTHER MAJOR FIGURES	Brigham Young (1801–1877) Sidney Rigdon (1793–1876)	Hiram Edson (1806–1892) Joseph Bates (1792–1872) Ellen G. White (1827–1915)		Phineas P. Quimby (1802–1866)	Joseph F. Rutherford (1869–1942) Nathan H. Knorr (1905–1977) Frederick Franz (1895–1992)
EXTRABIBLICAL SOURCES OF AUTHORITY	*Book of Mormon Doctrine and Covenants Pearl of Great Price* Ongoing divine revelation through president of church	Writings of Ellen G. White Continuing gift of prophecy within the church		*Science and Health with Key to the Scriptures*	*New World Translation of the Holy Scriptures* Writings produced by Brooklyn, NY, headquarters
DOCTRINE OF GOD	Polytheism – God was once man, man becomes god. God has a body.	Orthodox		Pantheism – All is God. Matter does not exist.	Monotheism – Doctrine of the Trinity denied.
PERSON OF CHRIST	Christ is divine, but not unique.	Orthodox		Distinguish between Jesus (a man) and Christ (a divine idea) cf. Gnosticism.	Arian – Christ is unique but not divine, identified with Michael the Archangel, the first created being.
WORK OF CHRIST	Death of Christ erased effect of Adam's sin, thus providing for the resurrection of all people.	Atonement is substitutionary but not finished; Investigative Judgment is now determining whose sins are to be blotted out.		Christ was the great example of a scientific healing practitioner.	Ransom removes original sin from all "good and faithful" people, providing them with opportunity for everlasting life.

Chart 107

Major Nineteenth-Century American Cults (continued)

	MORMONS	ADVENTISTS	CHRISTIAN SCIENCE	JEHOVAH'S WITNESSES
HOLY SPIRIT	Impersonal force	Orthodox	Not distinguished from God	Impersonal force
MAN	Man was preexistent and has innate goodness.	Orthodox (dichotomist)	Man is coeternal with God. Bodies are nonexistent. Sin is imaginary.	Sin is not pervasive, merely an imperfection.
SALVATION	Comes through faith, repentance, baptism, laying on of hands, keeping commandments.	Comes through faith, keeping Mosaic law (especially Sabbath commandment).	Comes through realizing that sin and evil do not exist.	Comes through faith plus works to gain God's approval.
CHURCH	Exclusivist – After apostle John died, church ceased to exist until 1830; only their sacraments valid.	Formerly exclusivist – Now teach that all true believers will eventually keep the Ten Commandments.	Exclusivist	Exclusivist – All others will be annihilated.
INDIVIDUAL ESCHATOLOGY	There is a second chance after death; no eternal punishment; man eventually advances to godhood.	Soul sleep and annihilation of wicked are taught.	There is probation after death, allowing growth into truth; otherwise, annihilation.	Soul sleep and annihilation of wicked are taught.
GENERAL ESCHATOLOGY	Israel (American Indians) will be restored. Millennial reign of Christ will take place from Jerusalem and Independence, MO. All people will be assigned to one of three kingdoms, according to degree of spiritual advancement.	Hold premillennial, posttribulational views. Righteous will spend eternity on renewed earth.		Christ returned in 1914. Millennial Kingdom was to begin after Armageddon in 1975. The 144,000 will spend eternity in heaven; all other Witnesses in earthly Paradise.
PRACTICE	Practice abstinence from liquor, tobacco, coffee, tea. Fasting, tithing, Sabbath-keeping required. Marriage is for time and eternity. Encourage baptism for dead relatives.	Adhere to Old Testament dietary laws. Practice Sabbath-keeping, believers' baptism by immersion, foot-washing.	Have no sacraments. Church government and teaching cannot be changed without written permission from Mrs. Eddy. All churches are linked to the Mother Church in Boston.	Teach total pacifism. Refuse to participate in government (voting, holding office, saluting flag, taking oaths, national holidays, etc.). No blood transfusions are permitted.

Chart 107

Nineteenth- and Twentieth-Century Parachurch Organizations

ORGANIZATION	DATE OF FOUNDING	FOUNDER	NOTABLE FACTS
AMERICAN BIBLE SOCIETY	1816	John Jay Richard Varick	Formed for the purpose of disseminating the Scriptures widely in versions without annotations. In cooperation with other Bible Societies, has produced translations including the *Good News Bible* (*Good News for Modern Man*).
YOUNG MEN'S CHRISTIAN ASSOCIATION	1844	George Williams	Originally founded in Britain for the purpose of evangelistic outreach. Spread through British Empire and to the United States and France within a decade. Expanded to include relief and recreational work by turn of century.
YOUNG WOMEN'S CHRISTIAN ASSOCIATION	1855	Emma Roberts	Originally founded in Britain to reach young women for Christ. Experienced expansion and change similar to its male counterpart.
STUDENT VOLUNTEER MOVEMENT	1888	John R. Mott	Founded to recruit students on college campuses for the work of foreign missions. Encouraged in its early years by D. L. Moody. Merged into University Christian Movement, which became defunct in 1969.
INTERVARSITY CHRISTIAN FELLOWSHIP USA	1941	Stacey Woods	Originated in Britain to promote evangelism on college and university campuses. USA branch founded through assistance from Canada. Joined with other national Intervarsity branches to form International Fellowship of Evangelical Students.
NAVIGATORS	1943	Dawson Trotman	Formed to encourage evangelism, Bible study, and Bible memorization. Initially concentrated on members of the armed services, both in the United States and abroad. Now also works on college campuses and in the business community.
NATIONAL SUNDAY SCHOOL ASSOCIATION	1945	Henrietta Mears and others	Formed to promote and provide teaching materials for Sunday schools. Now a subsidiary of the National Association of Evangelicals.
YOUTH FOR CHRIST, INTERNATIONAL	1945	Torrey Johnson	Established to reach teenagers with the gospel. Conducts Bible clubs, youth rallies, and sponsors short-term mission trips. Organization with which Billy Graham got his start.
FULL GOSPEL BUSINESS MEN'S FELLOWSHIP, INTERNATIONAL	1951	Demos Shakarian	Pentecostal in emphasis. Attempts to reach out to people in the business community. Now has chapters all over the world.
CAMPUS CRUSADE FOR CHRIST	1951	William R. Bright	Founded to reach out to students on college campuses. Known for use of "Four Spiritual Laws" for evangelism. Now conducts work in foreign countries as well as in the United States.

Chart 108

Nineteenth-Century American Theologians and Preachers

NAME	DATES	REPRESENTATIVE WRITINGS	NOTABLE FACTS
ARCHIBALD ALEXANDER	1772–1851	*A Brief Outline of the Evidences of the Christian Religion*	President of Hampden-Sydney College 1796–1806. First president and professor at Princeton Theological Seminary from founding in 1812.
CHARLES HODGE	1797–1878	*Systematic Theology* *Commentary on the First Epistle to the Corinthians*	Studied and taught at Princeton Theological Seminary 1820–1878. Founded and edited *Princeton Review*. Leader of Old School Presbyterians. Espoused Scottish Common Sense Realism.
JAMES H. THORNWELL	1812–1862	*Lectures in Theology* Founder of the *Southern Presbyterian Review*	Taught at South Carolina College, Columbia Theological Seminary. Founder of Presbyterian Church in the Confederate States in 1861. Defended institution of slavery from Scripture.
HENRY WARD BEECHER	1813–1887	*Freedom and War* *Yale Lectures on Preaching* *Doctrinal Beliefs and Unbeliefs*	Son of Lyman Beecher, brother of Harriet Beecher Stowe; ardent abolitionist. One of the most popular preachers in America in his day. Became increasingly liberal, espoused higher criticism, evolution, Gospel of Wealth.
W. G. T. SHEDD	1820–1894	*Dogmatic Theology* *A History of Christian Doctrine*	Presbyterian theologian who taught at Auburn, Andover, and Union Theological Seminaries. Defended orthodox Calvinism in opposition to higher critical attacks by colleagues at Union.
ROBERT L. DABNEY	1820–1898	*Syllabus and Notes of the Course of Systematic and Polemic Theology*	Chaplain for Stonewall Jackson's army during the Civil War. Helped found Presbyterian Church in the Confederate States. Taught at Union Seminary (1853–1883) and Austin Theological Seminary (1883–1894). Attempted justification of slavery and later segregation.
A. A. HODGE	1823–1886	*Outlines of Theology* *The Life of Charles Hodge* *The Atonement*	Son of Charles Hodge Taught at Western Theological Seminary (1864–1877) and Princeton Theological Seminary (1878–1886).
WASHINGTON GLADDEN	1836–1918	Served as editor of the *Independent*	Leader in Social Gospel movement in America. Pastor of First Congregational Church in Columbus, OH 1882–1914. Tried to prevent denomination from accepting gift from Standard Oil.
AUGUSTUS H. STRONG	1836–1921	*Systematic Theology* *Christ in Creation and Ethical Monism*	Converted under preaching of Charles G. Finney. President of Rochester Theological Seminary 1872–1912. Personally orthodox, but drawn to German philosophy and theistic evolution. First president of the Northern Baptist Convention.
WALTER RAUSCHENBUSCH	1861–1918	*Christianity and the Social Crisis* *A Theology for the Social Gospel*	German Baptist pastor and professor of New Testament and Church History Father of the Social Gospel in America; espoused Christian socialism. Taught at Rochester Theological Seminary 1897–1918.

Chart 109

Late Nineteenth- and Early Twentieth-Century Revivalists

NAME	DATES	BIRTHPLACE	CHURCH AFFILIATION	SCHOOLS FOUNDED AND/OR TAUGHT AT	NOTABLE FACTS
DWIGHT L. MOODY	1837–1899	Northfield, MA	Independent	Northfield Seminary (school for girls; founder – 1879) Mt. Hermon School (school for boys; founder – 1881) Chicago Evangelization Society (now Moody Bible Institute; founder – 1886)	Dropped out of school in seventh grade. Was converted at age 18. Became shoe salesman in Boston, then Chicago. Began preaching among soldiers during Civil War. Gained prominence with 1873–1875 crusade in British Isles. Was never ordained. Held crusades all over America with Ira Sankey until his death in 1899.
SAMUEL PORTER JONES	1847–1906	Oak Bowery, AL	Methodist		Never attended college. Was converted after bout with alcoholism. Supported Prohibition. Became known as the "Moody of the South."
REUBEN A. TORREY	1856–1928	Hoboken, NJ	Congregational	Moody Bible Institute (president 1889–1908) Bible Institute of Los Angeles (now Biola University; dean 1912–1924)	Graduated from Yale College and Divinity School. Worked with Moody. Made several international preaching tours. Served as editor for *The Fundamentals*.
J. WILBUR CHAPMAN	1859–1918	Richmond, IN	Presbyterian		Attended Oberlin College, Lake Forest University, Lane Theological Seminary. Assisted Moody in some of his crusades. Was director of Winona Lake Bible Conference.
BILLY SUNDAY	1862–1935	Ames, IA	Presbyterian		Was professional baseball player, 1883–1891. Was converted through Pacific Garden Mission in Chicago in 1886. Assisted J. Wilbur Chapman in some of his crusades. Began independent crusades in 1896. Had a highly sensational, dramatic preaching style. Advocated temperance. Opposed theory of evolution.

Chart 110

Key Figures in the Dissemination of Dispensationalism in America

NAME	DATES	CHURCH AFFILIATION	REPRESENTATIVE WRITINGS	SCHOOLS FOUNDED AND/OR TAUGHT AT	NOTABLE FACTS
JOHN NELSON DARBY	1800–1882	Church of Ireland Plymouth Brethren	*On the Nature and Unity of the Church of Christ*		Studied law. Was ordained to priesthood in 1825. Was greatest popularizer of Plymouth Brethren. Visited America seven times.
JAMES H. BROOKES	1830–1897	Presbyterian	*Maranatha* *Israel and the Church* *Is the Bible Inspired?*		Organized Niagara Bible Conferences. Influenced Scofield. Studied at Miami University of Ohio, Princeton Theological Seminary. Served as pastor in Dayton and St. Louis.
WILLIAM E. BLACKSTONE	1841–1935	Methodist	*Jesus Is Coming*		Helped start Chicago Hebrew Mission. Supported Zionism. Has forest named after him in Israel.
CYRUS INGERSON SCOFIELD	1843–1921	Congregationalist	*Scofield Reference Bible* *Rightly Dividing the Word of Truth*	Philadelphia School of the Bible (now Philadelphia Biblical University; helped found, 1914)	Served in Confederate army. Studied law. Served in Kansas House of Representatives. Was influenced by Brookes. Served as pastor in Dallas, TX and Northfield, MA. Founded Central American Mission. Spread dispensationalism through his annotated reference Bible.
ARNO C. GAEBELEIN	1861–1945	Methodist	*The Annotated Bible* *Revelation: An Analysis and Exposition* *Current Events in the Light of the Bible*		Was born in Germany. Founded and edited *Our Hope* magazine. Served as pastor in Baltimore, New York, Hoboken. Superintended Hope of Israel Mission.

Chart 111

NAME	DATES	CHURCH AFFILIATION	REPRESENTATIVE WRITINGS	SCHOOLS FOUNDED AND/OR TAUGHT AT	NOTABLE FACTS
LEWIS SPERRY CHAFER	1871–1952	Presbyterian	*Systematic Theology* *The Kingdom in History and Prophecy* *Major Bible Themes*	Philadelphia School of the Bible (now Philadelphia Biblical University; cofounder and teacher, 1914–1923) Dallas Theological Seminary (founder, teacher, and president, 1924–1952)	Studied music at Oberlin College. Taught at Mount Hermon School for Boys. Served as pastor at Scofield Memorial Church in Dallas. Edited *Bibliotheca Sacra*.
JOHN F. WALVOORD	1910–2002	Presbyterian	*The Rapture Question* *The Millennial Kingdom* *Armageddon, Oil, and the Middle East Crisis*	Dallas Theological Seminary (teacher, president, and chancellor, 1936–2001)	Born in Sheboygan, WI. Studied at Wheaton College and Dallas Theological Seminary. Taught Systematic Theology at Dallas. Became influential speaker and writer on matters of biblical prophecy. His book on the Middle East crisis was read by President George H. W. Bush prior to Desert Storm.

Chart 111

A Comparison of Historic Covenant and Historic Dispensational Theology

ISSUE	COVENANT POSITION	DISPENSATIONAL POSITION
PATTERN OF HISTORY	Covenant of Works with Adam; Covenant of Grace with Christ on behalf of the elect (some distinguish between Covenant of Redemption with Christ and Covenant of Grace with the elect).	Divided into dispensations (usually seven); e.g., Innocence (pre-Fall), Conscience (Adam), Human Government (Noah); Promise (Abraham), Law (Moses), Grace (Christ's First Coming), Kingdom (Christ's Second Coming).
VIEW OF HISTORY	Optimistic; God is extending his kingdom.	Pessimistic; the Last Days are marked by increasingly worse wickedness in the world and by apostasy in the church.
GOD'S PURPOSE IN HISTORY	There is a unified redemptive purpose.	There are two distinct purposes, one earthly (Israel), one heavenly (Church).
VIEW OF THE BIBLICAL COVENANTS	They are different administrations of the Covenant of Grace.	They mark off periods of time during which God's specific demands of man differ.
RELATIONSHIP OF OLD TESTAMENT TO NEW TESTAMENT	Acceptance of Old Testament teaching required unless specifically abrogated by New Testament.	Old Testament prescriptions are not binding unless reaffirmed in New Testament.
RELATIONSHIP BETWEEN ISRAEL AND THE CHURCH	The church is spiritual Israel, in continuity with true Israel of Old Testament.	The church is the spiritual people of God, distinct from Israel, the physical people of God.
OLD TESTAMENT PROPHECY	Refers to God's people, the church.	Refers to ethnic Israel.
CHURCH AGE	God's redemptive purpose continues to unfold.	There is a parenthesis between past and future manifestations of the kingdom.
ROLE OF THE HOLY SPIRIT	The Holy Spirit indwells God's people throughout history.	The Holy Spirit indwells God's people only from Pentecost to the Rapture.
BAPTISM	Unified covenant generally used to support infant baptism by analogy with circumcision.	Israel/Church distinction often (but not always) used to support believers' baptism.
SOCIAL IMPLICATIONS	Emphasizes "Cultural Mandate."	The only way to save the world is to save individuals, therefore evangelism takes precedence over "social action."
ESCHATOLOGY	Usually amillennial; rarely postmillennial; occasionally premillennial.	Premillennial, usually pretribulational.
MILLENNIUM	Symbolic, often identified with present age.	Literal, earthly 1,000-year reign after Second Coming.

Chart 112

Denominational Divisions over the Modernist-Fundamentalist Controversy

DENOMINATION	YEAR OF DIVISION	SECEDING GROUP	NATURE OF SECEDING GROUP	KEY FIGURES CONSERVATIVE	KEY FIGURES LIBERAL
DISCIPLES OF CHRIST	1927	Christian Churches; Churches of Christ	Conservative	John W. McGarvey R. C. Foster P. H. Welshimer	James H. Garrison Herbert L. Willett C. C. Morrison
NORTHERN BAPTIST CONVENTION (now American Baptist Convention)	1932	General Association of Regular Baptists	Conservative	John Roach Straton Jasper C. Massee Amzi C. Dixon William Bell Riley Chester Tulga Robert Ketcham	Walter Rauschenbusch Harry Emerson Fosdick
	1947	Conservative Baptist Association	Conservative		
PRESBYTERIAN CHURCH IN THE UNITED STATES OF AMERICA	1936	Orthodox Presbyterian Church	Conservative	J. Gresham Machen Paul Woolley	J. Ross Stevenson Henry Sloan Coffin
PRESBYTERIAN CHURCH IN THE UNITED STATES	1973	Presbyterian Church in America	Conservative	G. Aiken Taylor	
LUTHERAN CHURCH, MISSOURI SYNOD	1976	Association of Evangelical Lutherans	Liberal	Jacob A. O. Preus Ralph Bohlmann	John Tietjen Arlis Ehlen

Chart 113

Key Figures in the Twentieth-Century Presbyterian Schisms

NAME	DATES	SCHOOLS FOUNDED AND/OR TAUGHT AT	REPRESENTATIVE WRITINGS	NOTABLE FACTS
CHARLES A. BRIGGS	1841–1913	Union Theological Seminary (taught 1874–1913)	*Hebrew and English Lexicon of the Old Testament* *Critical and Exegetical Commentary on the Book of Psalms*	Studied at University of Virginia, Union Theological Seminary, University of Berlin. In 1893 was suspended from Presbyterian Church for denying inspiration of Scripture. In 1900 was ordained in Episcopal Church. Was first editor of *International Critical Commentary* series.
HENRY PRESERVED SMITH	1847–1927	Lane Theological Seminary (taught 1874–1894) Amherst (1898–1907) Meadville Theological School (1907–1913) Union Theological Seminary (1913–1925)	*The Religion of Israel* *Essays in Biblical Interpretation*	Studied at Amherst, Lane, Berlin. In 1894 was suspended for heresy for defending Briggs.
BENJAMIN B. WARFIELD	1851–1921	Western Theological Seminary (taught 1878–1887) Princeton Theological Seminary (1887–1921)	*The Plan of Salvation* *Counterfeit Miracles* *Revelation and Inspiration* *Perfectionism*	Studied at Princeton University and Seminary. Was major opponent of Briggs and Smith. Maintained continuity of Princeton Theology from Hodges. Edited *Princeton Theological Review.*
ROBERT DICK WILSON	1856–1930	Western Theological Seminary (taught 1880–1881, 1883–1900) Princeton Theological Seminary (1900–1929) Westminster Theological Seminary (cofounded and taught 1929–1930)	*Hebrew Grammar for Beginners* *Studies in the Book of Daniel* *Scientific Investigation of the Old Testament*	Was notable philologist and Old Testament scholar. Opposed higher criticism, defended authenticity of Old Testament documents.
HENRY SLOAN COFFIN	1877–1954	Union Theological Seminary (taught 1905–1945; president from 1926)	*In a Day of Social Rebuilding* *The Meaning of the Cross*	Wrote Auburn Affirmation. Studied at Yale, Edinburgh, Union Theological Seminary. Advocated Social Gospel. Was involved in ecumenism.

Chart 114

NAME	DATES	SCHOOLS FOUNDED AND/OR TAUGHT AT	REPRESENTATIVE WRITINGS	NOTABLE FACTS
HARRY EMERSON FOSDICK	1878–1969	Union Theological Seminary (taught 1909–1946)	*The Modern Use of the Bible* *A Guide to Understanding the Bible*	As liberal Baptist preacher stirred controversy in Presbyterian Church. Was pastor of Riverside Church in New York. Helped draft Auburn Affirmation. Opposed Fundamentalism.
J. GRESHAM MACHEN	1881–1937	Princeton Theological Seminary (taught 1906–1929) Westminster Theological Seminary (founded, taught, president 1929–1937)	*Christianity and Liberalism* *The Virgin Birth* *The Origin of Paul's Religion*	Studied at Johns Hopkins, Princeton University and Seminary. Founded Independent Board of Presbyterian Foreign Missions. Was defrocked for insubordination in 1935. Was leading founder of Orthodox Presbyterian Church.
J. OLIVER BUSWELL	1895–1977	Wheaton College (president 1926–1939) Faith Theological Seminary (taught 1939–1940) Shelton College (taught 1941–1955) Covenant Theological Seminary (taught 1956–1969)	*A Systematic Theology of the Christian Religion*	Studied at University of Minnesota, McCormick Theological Seminary, New York University. Served as army chaplain during World War I. Was involved in schisms in 1936, 1937, 1956.
ALLAN MacRAE	1902–1997	Westminster Theological Seminary (taught 1929–1937) Faith Theological Seminary (president 1937–1971) Biblical Theological Seminary (president 1971–1983)	*The Gospel of Isaiah*	Studied at Occidental College, Bible Institute of Los Angeles (Biola), Princeton Theological Seminary, University of Berlin. Was involved in schisms in 1936, 1937. Was editor of *New Scofield Reference Bible*. Served on translation team for *New International Version*.
CARL McINTIRE	1906–2002	Faith Theological Seminary (founded 1937) Shelton College (founded 1941)		Was involved in schisms in 1936, 1937, 1956. Founded Bible Presbyterian Church (1937). Founded American Council of Christian Churches to oppose National Council of Churches. Founded International Council of Christian Churches to oppose World Council of Churches. Supported Vietnam War with marches on Washington.

Chart 114

Twentieth-Century American Theologians and Preachers

NAME	DATES	REPRESENTATIVE WRITINGS	NOTABLE FACTS
GEERHARDUS VOS	1862–1949	*Biblical Theology* *Pauline Eschatology*	Born in the Netherlands, but educated in Germany and the United States. Taught at Princeton Theological Seminary 1893–1932. Did groundbreaking work in the field of Biblical Theology.
LOUIS BERKHOF	1873–1957	*Reformed Dogmatics* *The History of Christian Doctrine*	Born in the Netherlands, educated at Calvin Seminary. Professor and president of Calvin Seminary 1906–1957. One of the leading Reformed theologians of the twentieth century.
OSWALD T. ALLIS	1880–1973	*The Five Books of Moses* *The Unity of Isaiah*	Taught at Princeton Theological Seminary (1918–1929) and Westminster Theological Seminary (1929–1936); edited *Princeton Theological Review*. Defended orthodox view of Scripture in opposition to liberal criticism, gave classic argument against Wellhausen's Documentary Hypothesis.
REINHOLD NIEBUHR	1892–1971	*Moral Man and Immoral Society* *Faith and History*	Taught at Union Theological Seminary 1928–1960. Influenced by Barth's Neo-Orthodoxy. Founder and editor of periodical *Christianity and Crisis* 1941–1966.
H. RICHARD NIEBUHR	1894–1962	*Social Sources of Denominationalism* *Christ and Culture*	Neo-Orthodox theologian and brother of Reinhold Niebuhr Taught Christian Ethics at Yale Divinity School 1931–1962. Emphasized need for Christianity to have an impact on the larger society.
CORNELIUS VAN TIL	1895–1987	*Defense of the Faith* *A Christian Theory of Knowledge*	Taught Apologetics at Westminster Theological Seminary from its inception in 1929. Originator of presuppositional apologetics. Opposed both Neo-Orthodoxy and liberalism as departures from biblical Christianity.
JOHN MURRAY	1898–1975	*Principles of Conduct* *Redemption Accomplished and Applied*	Professor of Systematic Theology at Princeton Theological Seminary and Westminster Theological Seminary.
GORDON H. CLARK	1902–1985	*Thales to Dewey* *Religion, Reason, and Revelation*	Taught at University of Pennsylvania, Wheaton College (1936–1943), and Butler University (1945–1973). After conflict in Orthodox Presbyterian Church, joined Reformed Presbyterian Church, Evangelical Synod. Philosophy sometimes described as Christian Rationalism.
JOHN COURTNEY MURRAY	1904–1967	*We Hold These Truths* *The Problem of God, Yesterday and Today*	Jesuit and leading American Catholic theologian of the 20th century Taught at Woodstock Seminary 1937–1967. Wrote Vatican II document on Religious Freedom, sought to reconcile Catholicism and democracy.

Chart 115

NAME	DATES	REPRESENTATIVE WRITINGS	NOTABLE FACTS
FRANCIS SCHAEFFER	1912–1985	*Escape from Reason* *The God Who Is There* *How Should We Then Live?*	Presbyterian pastor, studied under Cornelius Van Til. Founder of L'Abri Fellowship, ministry to intellectuals in Swiss Alps. Greatest popularizer of presuppositional apologetics. Popular speaker on college campuses.
CARL F. H. HENRY	1913–2003	*The Uneasy Conscience of Modern Fundamentalism* *God, Revelation, and Authority*	Most widely respected of 20th-century evangelical theologians. Helped found Evangelical Theological Society, Fuller Theological Seminary. Opposed theological subjectivism of both Neo-Orthodoxy and fundamentalism. Built apologetic around Law of Non-Contradiction and analysis of presuppositions.
BILLY GRAHAM	b.1918	*Peace With God* *World Aflame*	Southern Baptist evangelist who has preached gospel to more people than anyone in history. Founded Billy Graham Evangelistic Association, *Christianity Today* and *Decision* magazines. Pioneered use of television and movies to spread the gospel.
EDWARD J. CARNELL	1919–1967	*An Introduction to Christian Apologetics* *A Philosophy of the Christian Religion*	Studied under Gordon Clark at Wheaton College. Professor (1947–1967) and president (1954–1959) at Fuller Theological Seminary. Developed philosophical defense of Christian faith against liberal attacks. Became highly critical of the fundamentalism in which he was raised.
JOHN MEYENDORFF	1926–1992	*Byzantine Theology* *Byzantium and the Rise of Russia*	Born in France to Russian parents, emigrated to United States in 1959. Leading Orthodox theologian in 20th-century America. Taught at St. Vladimir's Orthodox Theological Seminary, dean there from 1984.
MARTIN LUTHER KING JR.	1929–1968	*Stride Toward Freedom* *Why We Can't Wait*	Baptist pastor, most visible leader of the Civil Rights Movement. Founder and first president of Southern Christian Leadership Conference. Won Nobel Peace Prize in 1964.
ALVIN PLANTINGA	b.1932	*God, Freedom, and Evil* *Does God Have a Nature?*	Professor at Calvin College (1963–1982), Notre Dame University (from 1982). Favors Ontological Argument for God's existence. Develops Christian epistemology in his writings.
JERRY FALWELL	b.1933	*Strength for the Journey* *The New American Family*	Pastor of Thomas Road Baptist Church in Lynchburg, VA. Founder of Liberty University and the Moral Majority.
JAMES M. BOICE	1938–2000	*Foundations of the Christian Faith*	Pastor of Tenth Presbyterian Church in Philadelphia. Chaired International Council on Biblical Inerrancy 1977–1987.
JAMES H. CONE	b.1938	*A Black Theology of Liberation* *God of the Oppressed*	Came to public attention as theologian of Black Power. Professor at Union Theological Seminary since 1976.

Chart 115

Leading Figures of the Pentecostal and Charismatic Movements

NAME	DATES	NOTABLE FACTS
ALMA WHITE	1862–1946	Founder of Pillar of Fire Organized camp meetings and preached revivals, causing conflict with Methodist Church. Left Methodists, formed Pentecostal Union (1901), which was later renamed Pillar of Fire.
WILLIAM J. SEYMOUR	1870–1922	Studied under Charles Parham in a Bible school in Houston, learning of the gift of tongues there. Moved to Los Angeles, led Azusa Street Revival 1906–1908. Founded newspaper, *The Apostolic Faith*.
CHARLES F. PARHAM	1873–1929	Methodist pastor and founder of modern American Pentecostalism Operated Bible schools in Topeka, KS, and Houston, TX. Glossolalia appeared at a Watchnight service on January 1, 1901, in Topeka when a student, Agnes Ozman, spoke in tongues.
AIMEE SEMPLE McPHERSON	1890–1944	Itinerant revival preacher after World War I, pioneer in radio evangelism Pastored Los Angeles Temple after leaving itinerant ministry. Founded International Church of the Foursquare Gospel.
DAVID DU PLESSIS	1905–1987	South African Assemblies of God pastor and one of the first worldwide figures in the Pentecostal Movement Active in World Council of Churches Attended Second Vatican Council as a Protestant observer.
KATHRYN KUHLMANN	c.1910–1976	Itinerant evangelist whose ministry expanded into radio and television Best known for her faith healing services
DEMOS SHAKARIAN	1913–1996	Of Armenian extraction, received filling of the Spirit at age 13. Entered career as a dairy farmer. Founded Full Gospel Business Men's Fellowship International in 1951.
DENNIS BENNETT	1917–1991	Pastor of St. Mark's Episcopal Church in Van Nuys, CA Initiated Charismatic Movement when people in his church received the baptism of the Holy Spirit and began speaking in tongues in 1960.
ORAL ROBERTS	b.1918	Miraculously healed of tuberculosis in his youth. Operates influential radio and television ministries emphasizing divine healing. Founder of Oral Roberts University, which includes a medical school

Chart 116

NAME	DATES	NOTABLE FACTS
CHUCK SMITH	b.1927	Originally sought to evangelize hippies and surfers in the 1960s. Founder of Calvary Chapel in Costa Mesa, CA in 1965 There are presently over 1000 Calvary Chapels worldwide, along with a Bible college in Costa Mesa.
PAT ROBERTSON	b.1930	Attended Yale Law School and New York Theological Seminary. Founder of the Christian Broadcasting Network and *The 700 Club* Ran for President in 1988.
JOHN WIMBER	1934–1997	Former rock musician converted at age 29 Became itinerant evangelist and healer, later a pastor. Founder of the Vineyard Movement

Chart 116

Pentecostals and Charismatics—A Comparison

	PENTECOSTALS	CHARISMATICS
MOVEMENT BEGAN	1900	1960
ROOTS	Holiness Movement in Methodism	Mainline Protestantism "Jesus Movement"
PIONEER FIGURE	Charles F. Parham	Dennis Bennett
SOCIAL MILIEU	Rural and urban poor	Suburban middle class
RELATIONSHIP TO CHURCH	Formed independent churches, later denominations.	Began with Bible studies in mainline churches, later formed independent congregations.
THEOLOGICAL DISTINCTIVES	Perfectionism, second blessing in common with evangelical Methodism	None – Initially maintained doctrine of churches in which Bible studies began (including Catholicism).
NATURE OF TONGUES	Initially thought to be foreign languages for missionary purposes, later understood as ecstatic speech.	Ecstatic speech
PURPOSE OF TONGUES	Communication of divine revelation, sign of second blessing	Communication of divine revelation, "prayer language"
COMMON CHARACTERISTICS	Speaking in tongues associated with the baptism of the Holy Spirit Emphasis on divine healing Continuation of gift of prophecy in the church Emphasis on experiential Christianity more than doctrine Emphasis on lively multisensory worship experience	

Chart 117

An American Presbyterian Family Tree

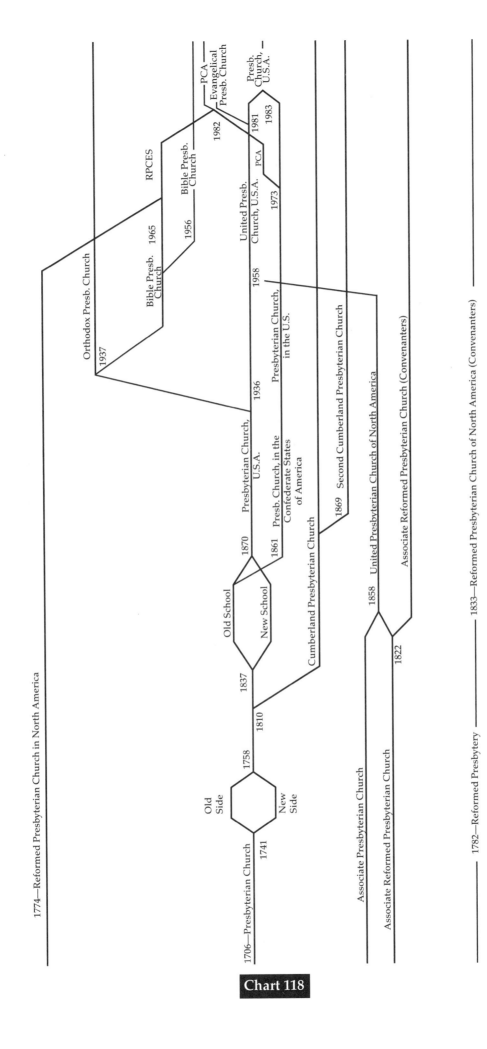

Chart 118

An American Baptist Family Tree

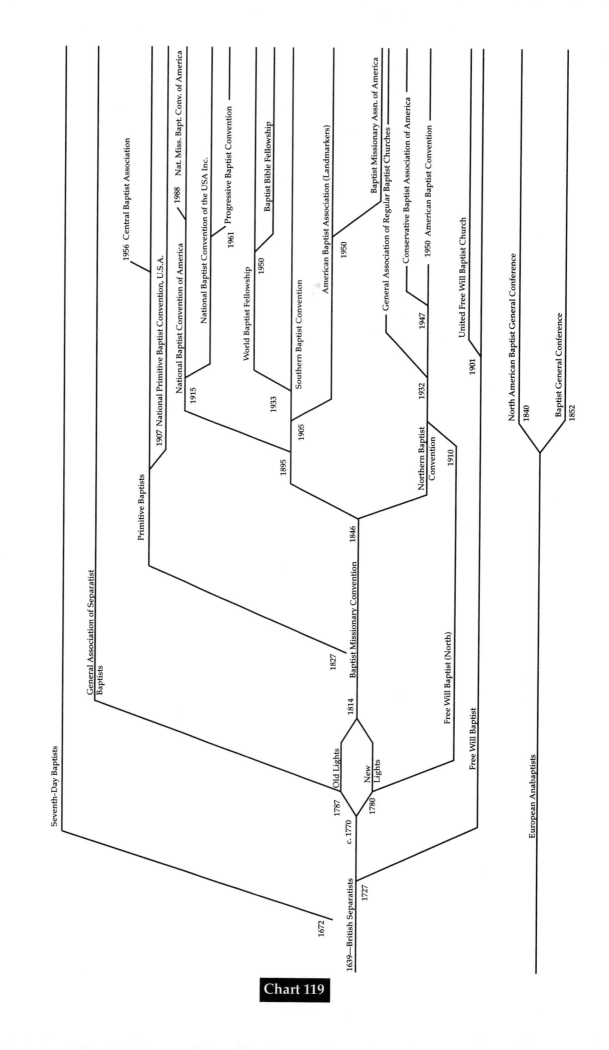

Chart 119

An American Lutheran Family Tree

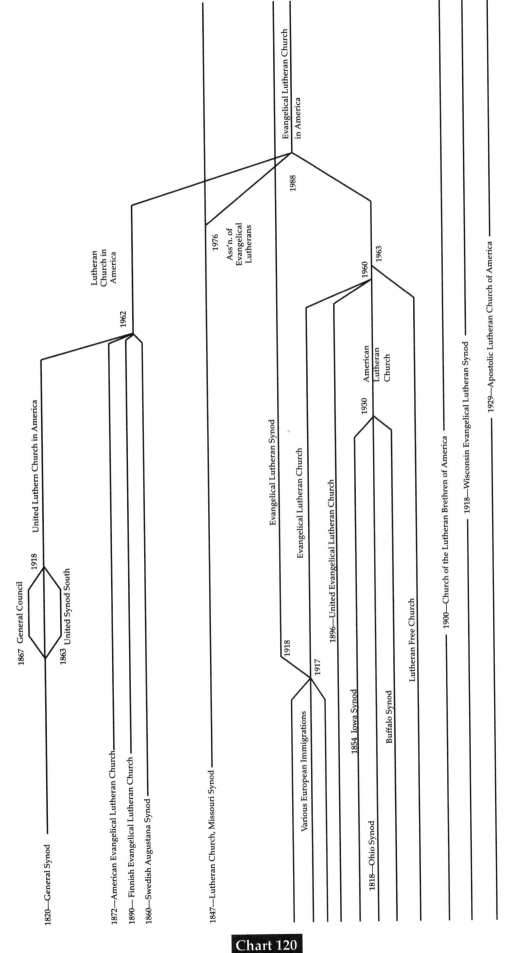

Chart 120

An American Episcopal Family Tree

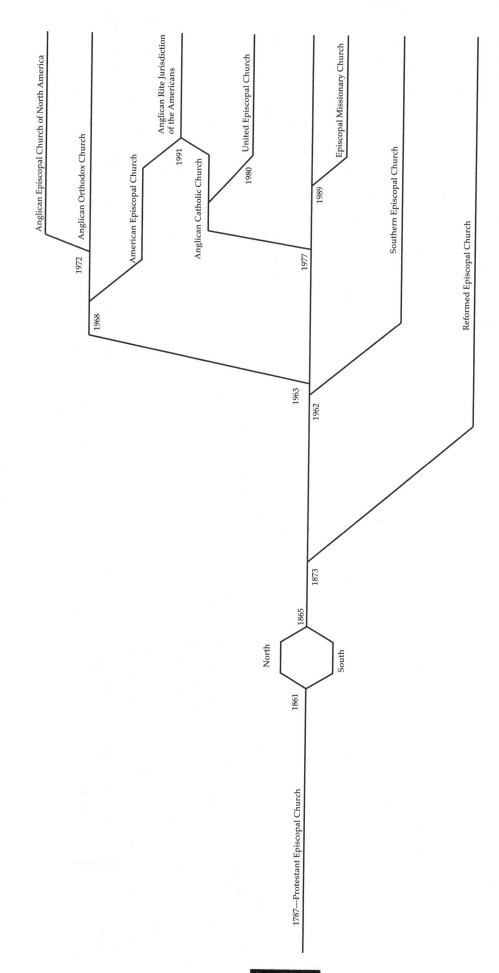

Anglican Episcopal Church of North America

Anglican Orthodox Church

American Episcopal Church

Anglican Rite Jurisdiction of the Americans

Anglican Catholic Church

United Episcopal Church

Episcopal Missionary Church

Southern Episcopal Church

Reformed Episcopal Church

1972

1991

1968

1980

1989

1977

1963

1962

1873

1865

North

South

1861

1787—Protestant Episcopal Church

Chart 121

An American Methodist Family Tree

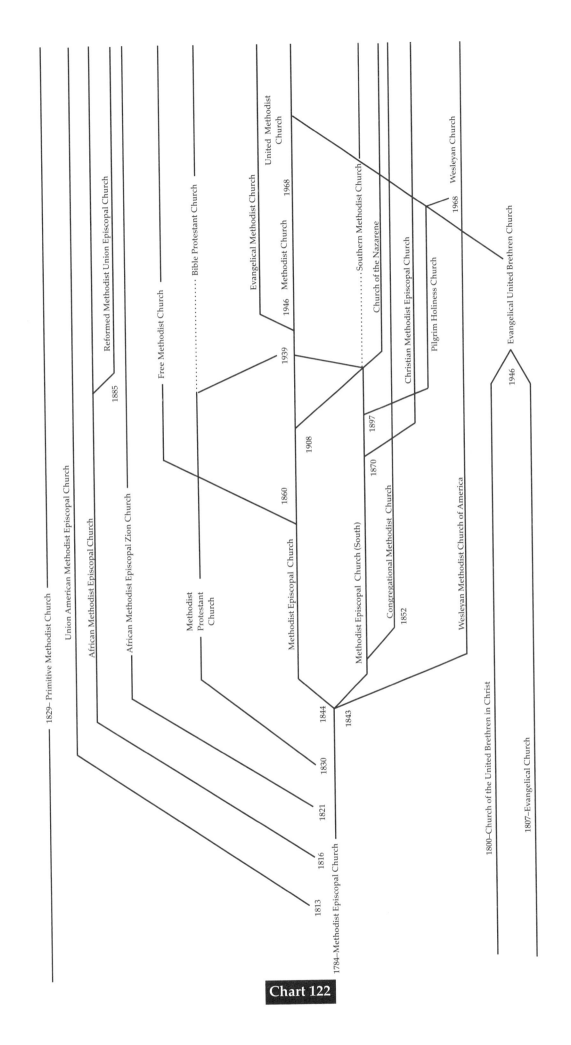

1829– Primitive Methodist Church

Union American Methodist Episcopal Church

African Methodist Episcopal Church

African Methodist Episcopal Zion Church

Reformed Methodist Union Episcopal Church — 1885

Free Methodist Church

Methodist Protestant Church

Bible Protestant Church

Evangelical Methodist Church

United Methodist Church

Methodist Church — 1968

1946

1939

1860

1908

Southern Methodist Church

Church of the Nazarene

Christian Methodist Episcopal Church

Pilgrim Holiness Church

Wesleyan Church — 1968

Methodist Episcopal Church

Methodist Episcopal Church (South)

Congregational Methodist Church — 1852

Wesleyan Methodist Church of America

Evangelical United Brethren Church — 1946

1897

1870

1844

1843

1830

1821

1816

1813

1784– Methodist Episcopal Church

1800– Church of the United Brethren in Christ

1807– Evangelical Church

Chart 122

An American Reformed and Congregationalist Family Tree

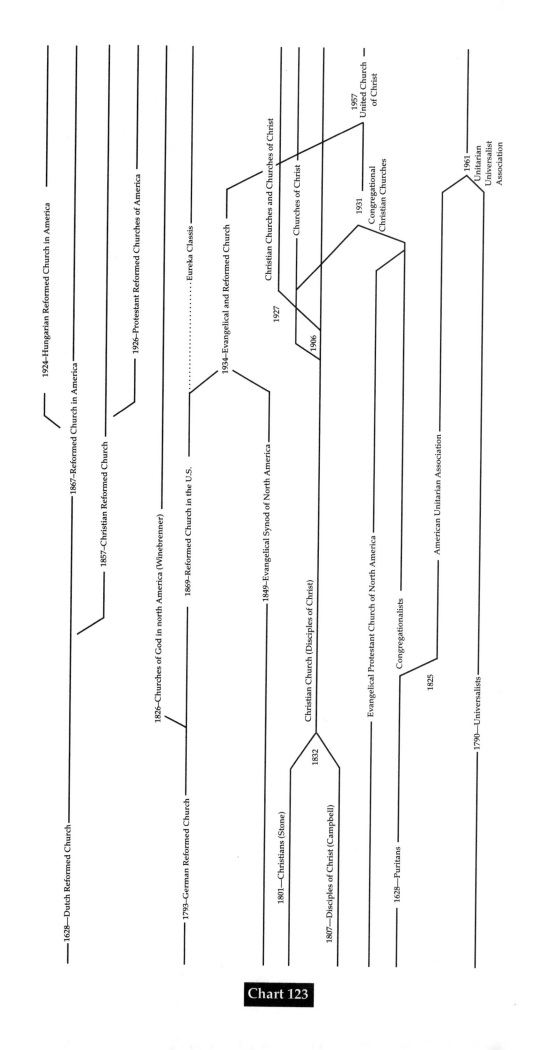

1628—Dutch Reformed Church

1924—Hungarian Reformed Church in America

1867—Reformed Church in America

1857—Christian Reformed Church

1826—Churches of God in north America (Winebrenner)

1926—Protestant Reformed Churches of America

1793—German Reformed Church

1869—Reformed Church in the U.S. .... Eureka Classis

1934—Evangelical and Reformed Church

1849—Evangelical Synod of North America

Christian Churches and Churches of Christ

1927

Churches of Christ

1906

Christian Church (Disciples of Christ)

1801—Christians (Stone)

1832

1807—Disciples of Christ (Campbell)

1957 United Church of Christ

1931 Congregational Christian Churches

Evangelical Protestant Church of North America

Congregationalists

1628—Puritans

1825

American Unitarian Association

1961 Unitarian Universalist Association

1790—Universalists

Chart 123

An American Pentecostal Family Tree

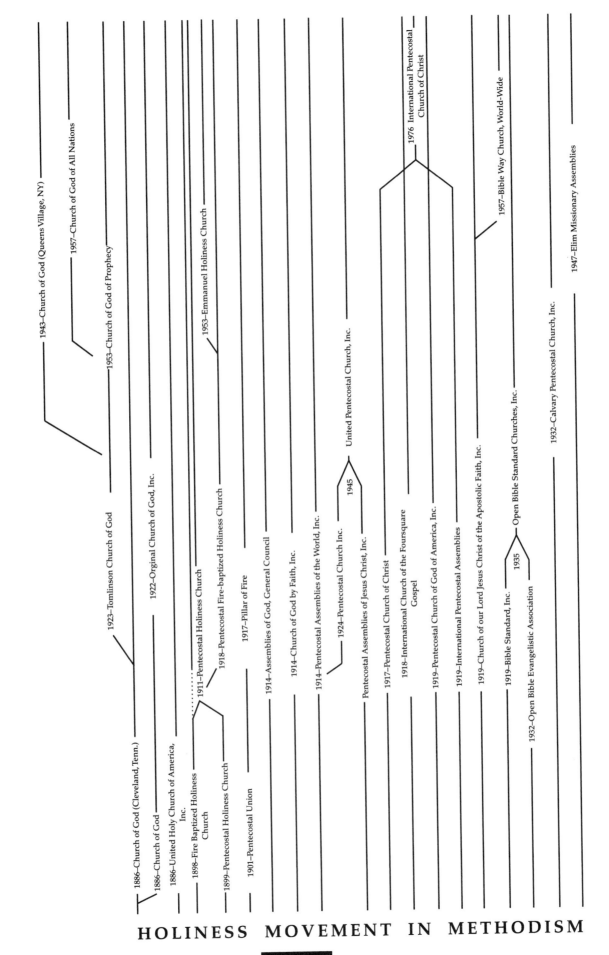

1886–Church of God (Cleveland, Tenn.)

1886–Church of God

1886–United Holy Church of America, Inc.

1898–Fire Baptized Holiness Church

1899–Pentecostal Holiness Church

1901–Pentecostal Union

1923–Tomlinson Church of God

1922–Orginal Church of God, Inc.

1911–Pentecostal Holiness Church

1918–Pentecostal Fire-baptized Holiness Church

1917–Pillar of Fire

1914–Assemblies of God, General Council

1914–Church of God by Faith, Inc.

1914–Pentecostal Assemblies of the World, Inc.

1924–Pentecostal Church Inc.

Pentecostal Assemblies of Jesus Christ, Inc.

1917–Pentecostal Church of Christ

1918–International Church of the Foursquare Gospel

1919–Pentecostal Church of God of America, Inc.

1919–International Pentecostal Assemblies

1919–Church of our Lord Jesus Christ of the Apostolic Faith, Inc.

1919–Bible Standard, Inc.

1935

Open Bible Standard Churches, Inc.

1932–Open Bible Evangelistic Association

1932–Calvary Pentecostal Church, Inc.

1943–Church of God (Queens Village, NY)

1957–Church of God of All Nations

1953–Church of God of Prophecy

1953–Emmanuel Holiness Church

United Pentecostal Church, Inc.

1945

1976 International Pentecostal Church of Christ

1957–Bible Way Church, World-Wide

1947–Elim Missionary Assemblies

HOLINESS MOVEMENT IN METHODISM

Chart 124

An American Mennonite Family Tree

1683–Mennonite Church

1859

1872

Old Order (Wisler) Mennonite Church

Church of God in Christ (Mennonite)

Old Order Amish Mennonite Church

1910

1927

Conservative Amish Mennonite Church

Beachy Amish Mennonite Churches

1954–Conservative Mennonite Conference

1874 - Hutterian Brethren

1812–Reformed Mennonite Church

1860–General Conference Mennonite Church

1865–Defenseless Mennonite Church

Conference of the Evangelical Mennonite Church

1876–Mennonite Brethren Church of North America

1889–Evangelical Mennonite Brethren

Fellowship of Evangelical Bible Churches

Chart 125

An American Adventist Family Tree

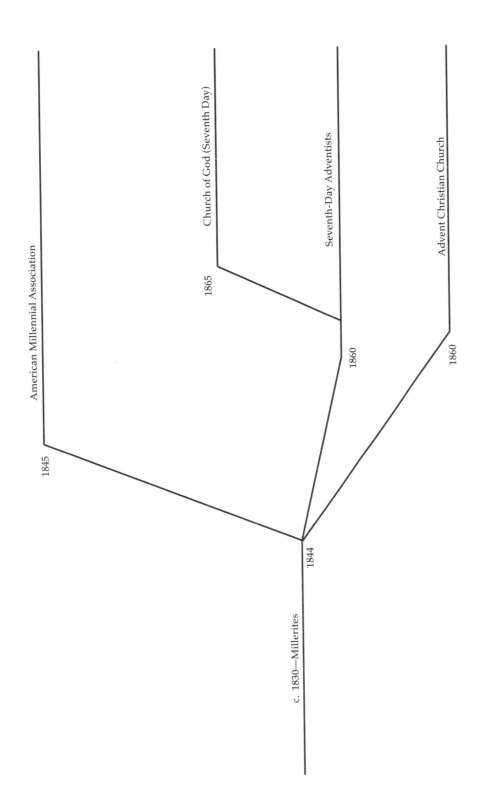

American Millennial Association

1845

Church of God (Seventh Day)

1865

Seventh-Day Adventists

1860

Advent Christian Church

1860

1844

c. 1830—Millerites

Chart 126

Bibliography

Abbott, Walter M., ed. *The Documents of Vatican II*. New York: Guild, 1966.

Ahlstrom, Sydney E. *A Religious History of the American People*. Garden City, NY: Doubleday, Image, 1975.

Alexander, Archibald. *The Log College*. London: Banner of Truth, 1968.

Alexander, David, and Patricia Alexander, eds. *Eerdmans' Handbook to the Bible*. Grand Rapids: Eerdmans, 1973.

Aquinas, Thomas. *Summa Theologica*. New York: Benziger Brothers, 1947.

Arnold, Eberhard. *The Early Christians after the Death of the Apostles*. Rifton, NY: Plough, 1970.

Ayer, Joseph Cullen. *A Source Book for Ancient Church History*. New York: Scribner, 1913.

Bainton, Roland H. *Here I Stand*. New York: New American Library, 1950.

————. *The Reformation of the Sixteenth Century*. Boston: Beacon, 1952.

Berkhof, Louis. *The History of Christian Doctrines*. Grand Rapids: Baker, 1976.

Berry, W. Grinton, ed. *Foxe's Book of Martyrs*. Grand Rapids: Baker, 1978.

Boer, Harry R. *A Short History of the Early Church*. Grand Rapids: Eerdmans, 1976.

Brauer, Jerald C. *Protestantism in America*. Philadelphia: Westminster, 1953.

————, ed. *The Westminster Dictionary of Church History*. Philadelphia: Westminster, 1971.

Bromiley, Geoffrey W. *Historical Theology: An Introduction*. Grand Rapids: Eerdmans, 1978.

Bruce, F. F. *The Spreading Flame*. Grand Rapids: Eerdmans, 1979.

Cairns, Earle E. *Christianity through the Centuries*. Grand Rapids: Zondervan, 1981.

Cantor, Norman F., ed. *The Medieval World: 300–1300*. New York: Macmillan, 1963.

Chadwick, Henry. *The Early Church*. Harmondsworth, Middlesex, England: Penguin, 1967.

Chadwick, Owen. *The Reformation*. Harmondsworth, Middlesex, England: Penguin, 1964.

Corbett, James A. *The Papacy: A Brief History*. Princeton, NJ: Van Nostrand, 1956.

Coulson, John, ed. *The Saints*. New York: Guild, 1958.

Cragg, Gerald R. *The Church and the Age of Reason 1618–1788*. Harmondsworth, Middlesex, England: Penguin, 1970.

Cross, F. L., and E. A. Livingstone, eds. *The Oxford Dictionary of the Christian Church*, 2nd ed. New York: Oxford University Press, 1983.

Dallimore, Arnold A. *George Whitefield*. Westchester, IL: Simon and Schuster, Cornerstone, 1979.

D'Aubigné, J. H. Merle. *The Life and Times of Martin Luther*. Chicago: Moody, 1978.

Dickens, A. G. *The Counter Reformation*. New York: Harcourt, Brace, and World, 1969.

————. *Reformation and Society in Sixteenth-Century Europe*. New York: Harcourt, Brace, and World, 1966.

Dolan, John P. *History of the Reformation*. New York: New American Library, 1965.

Douglas, J. D., ed. *The New International Dictionary of the Christian Church*. Grand Rapids: Zondervan, 1974.

Dowley, Tim, ed. *Eerdmans' Handbook to the History of Christianity*. Grand Rapids: Eerdmans, 1977.

Durant, Will. *The Age of Faith*. New York: Simon and Schuster, 1950.

————. *Caesar and Christ*. New York: Simon and Schuster, 1944.

————. *The Reformation*. New York: Simon and Schuster, 1957.

————. *The Renaissance*. New York: Simon and Schuster, 1953.

Elton, G. R., ed. *Renaissance and Reformation: 1300–1648*. New York: Macmillan, 1963.

Estep, William R. *The Anabaptist Story*. Grand Rapids: Eerdmans, 1975.

The Family Tree: A Chart of Protestant Denominations in the United States. Philadelphia: *Eternity* magazine, 1983.

Farrar, Frederic W. *Lives of the Fathers*. New York: Macmillan, 1889.

Ferguson, George. *Signs and Symbols in Christian Art*. New York: Oxford University Press, 1954.

Fleming, William. *Arts and Ideas*, 9th ed. Fort Worth: Harcourt Brace, 1995.

Foster, Richard J. *Streams of Living Water*. San Francisco: HarperCollins, 1998.

Fremantle, Anne, ed. *A Treasury of Early Christianity*. New York: New American Library, 1953.

Gaines, David P. *The World Council of Churches*. Peterborough, NH: Richard R. Smith, 1966.

Gaustad, Edwin Scott. *A Religious History of America*. New York: Harper and Row, 1974.

Glover, Robert H. *The Progress of World-Wide Missions*. New York: Harper and Row, 1960.

Gray, Janet Glenn. *The French Huguenots*. Grand Rapids: Baker, 1981.

Groves, C. P. *The Planting of Christianity in Africa*. London: Lutterworth, 1955.

Hawes, Stephen. *Synchronology of the Principal Events in Sacred and Profane History from the Creation of Man to the Present Time*. Boston: Hawes, 1870.

Hay, Denys. *The Medieval Centuries*. New York: Harper and Row, 1964.

Hildebrand. Hans J., ed. *The Reformation*. Grand Rapids: Baker, 1978.

Houghton, S. M., ed. *Five Pioneer Missionaries*. London: Banner of Truth, 1965.

———. *Sketches from Church History*. Edinburgh: Banner of Truth, 1980.

Hughes, Philip. *A Popular History of the Reformation*. Garden City, NY: Doubleday, 1957.

Kelly, J. N. D. *Early Christian Doctrines*. San Francisco: Harper and Row, 1978.

Latourette, Kenneth Scott. *A History of Christianity*. New York: Harper and Row, 1953.

———. *A History of the Expansion of Christianity*. Grand Rapids: Zondervan, 1970.

Lebreton, Jules, and Jacques Zeiller. *The Triumph of Christianity*. New York: Collier, 1946.

McBirnie, William Steuart. *The Search for the Twelve Apostles*. Wheaton, IL: Tyndale, 1973.

McConnell, S. D. *History of the American Episcopal Church*. New York: Thomas Whittaker, 1890.

Mead, Frank S., and Samuel S. Hill. *Handbook of Denominations in the United States*, 10th ed. Nashville: Abingdon, 1995.

Miller, Perry, ed. *The American Puritans*. Garden City, NY: Doubleday, 1956.

Moyer, Elgin S. *The Wycliffe Biographical Dictionary of the Church*. Chicago: Moody, 1982.

Neill, Stephen. *A History of Christian Missions*. Harmondsworth, Middlesex, England: Penguin, 1964.

Neve, J. L. *Churches and Sects of Christendom*. Burlington, IA: Lutheran Literary Board, 1940.

Newman, A. *A Manual of Church History*. Philadelphia: The American Baptist Publication Society, 1931.

Newton, Eric, and William Neil. *2000 Years of Christian Art*. New York: Harper and Row, 1966.

Nichols, James Hastings. *History of Christianity 1650–1950*. New York: Ronald, 1956.

Noll, Mark A. *Christians in the American Revolution*. Washington, DC: Christian University Press, 1977.

Noll, Mark A., et al., eds. *Eerdmans' Handbook to Christianity in America*. Grand Rapids: Eerdmans, 1983.

Palmer, R. R., Joel Colton, and Lloyd Cramer. *A History of the Modern World*, 9th ed. New York: McGraw Hill, 2002.

Parker, Percy Livingstone, ed. *The Journal of John Wesley*. Chicago: Moody, n.d.

Renwick. A. M. *The Story of the Church*. Leicester, England: InterVarsity, 1958.

Ryle, J. C. *Christian Leaders of the 18th Century*. Edinburgh: Banner of Truth, 1978.

Schaff, Philip. *The Creeds of Christendom*. New York: Harper and Brothers, 1881.

———. *History of the Christian Church*. Grand Rapids: Eerdmans, 1910.

Smith, M. A. *From Christ to Constantine*. Downers Grove, IL: InterVarsity, 1971.

———. *The Church Under Siege*. Downers Grove, IL: InterVarsity, 1976.

Southern, R. W. *Western Society and the Church in the Middle Ages*. Harmondsworth, Middlesex, England: Penguin, 1970.

Sparks, Jack, ed. *The Apostolic Fathers*. Nashville: Thomas Nelson, 1978.

Spitz, Lewis W., ed. *The Protestant Reformation*. Englewood Cliffs, NJ: Prentice-Hall. 1966.

Steinberg, S. H. *Historical Tables*. London: Macmillan, 1939.

Sweet, William W. *The Story of Religion in America*. Grand Rapids: Baker, 1973.

Toulouse, Mark G., and James O. Duke, eds. *Makers of Christian Theology in America*. Nashville: Abingdon Press, 1997.

Van Baalen, Jan Karel. *The Chaos of Cults*. Grand Rapids: Eerdmans, 1962.

Vidler, Alec R. *The Church in an Age of Revolution*. Harmondsworth, Middlesex, England: Penguin, 1961.

Westcott, B. F. *A General Survey of the History of the Canon of the New Testament*. Grand Rapids: Baker, 1980.

Williams, George H. *The Radical Reformation*, 3rd ed. Kirksville, MO: 1992.

Workman, Herbert B. *Persecution in the Early Church*. London: Charles H. Kelly, 1906.

Index

(By Chart Number)

Abelard, Peter 1, 31, 40, 43, 44
Abernathy, Ralph 106
Abolitionism 83, 102, 104, 105
Adam of St. Victor 8
Addison, Joseph 8
Adoptionism 25, 34
Adrian I 35
Adrian VI 54
Aeterni Patris 89
Aggiornamento 89
Ahlstrom, Sydney 93, 95
Alais, Peace of 51, 79
Alaric 9
Alban 20
Albertus Magnus 40, 42, 43
Albigensians 19, 45, 47, 90
Alcuin 31, 35, 36
Aldersgate Street 74, 81
Alexander III 38, 47
Alexander V 46, 47
Alexander VI 31
Alexander, Archibald 95, 109
Alexander, Cecil F. 8
Alexander of Alexandria 21, 28
Alexander of Jerusalem 20
Alexius I Comnenus 33
Alexius II Angelus 33
Alford, Henry 92
Alleine, Joseph 52, 63
Allen, Richard 95, 106
Allis, Oswald T. 115
Alva, Duke of 53
Ama-Sirayeli 88
Amana Church Society 97
Amboise, Peace of 66
Amboise, Tumult of 51, 66
Ambrose 8, 9, 21, 29
American Bible Society 92, 102, 108
American Civil War 95, 105
American Council of Christian Churches 114
American Revolution 74, 94, 100, 101
Amish 58, 96, 125
Ammann, Jacob 58
Amyraldianism 4, 65, 67
Amyraut, Moses 4, 51, 65, 67
Anabaptists 2, 50, 55, 56, 58, 67, 73
Anacletus II 47
Andreae, Jacob 67
Andrew 10

Angelico, Fra 59
Anne 64
Anne of Austria 79
Anne of Cleves 60, 61, 62
Anne of Denmark 64
Anselm 1, 31, 40
Anthony of Thebes 1, 9, 29
Antoninus Pius 9, 13, 20
Apocrypha 70, 89
Apollinarianism 26, 28
Apollinarius 9, 21, 24, 26
Apostles' Creed 58
Apostolic Faith, The 116
Apostolic Succession 13, 19, 22, 23
Aquinas, Thomas 1, 31, 40, 41, 42, 43
Arbez, Edward P. 92
Arianism 21, 25, 33, 63, 77, 107
Aristides 14
Aristotle 40, 60
Arius 9, 21, 24, 25, 28
Arles, Council of (AD 314) 24
Arminianism 2, 4, 65, 67, 72, 81, 103
Arminius, Jacob 4, 53
Arndt, Johann 49
Arras, League of 69
Asbury, Francis 80, 94, 102, 103, 106
Askold 6
Athanasius 1, 9, 17, 21, 24, 28, 29
Athenagoras 14
Auburn Affirmation 95, 114
Augsburg Confession 49, 67
Augsburg, Diet of 67
Augsburg, Peace of 49, 69
Augustine of Canterbury 1, 31, 32
Augustine of Hippo 1, 4, 9, 19, 21, 24, 27, 29, 30, 42
Augustinianism 4, 27, 36
Augustinians 29, 42, 48, 55, 60, 61
Aurelian 9, 20
Azusa Street Revival 116

Babylonian Captivity 1, 31, 34, 43, 46
Backus, Isaac 94
Bacon, Francis 77

Bacon, Roger 42
Baldwin of Flanders 38
Baptist Union 4
Barclay, William 92
Barmen Declaration 75, 84
Barnabas 6
Barnabas of Alexandria 13
Baronius, Caesar 54
Barth, Karl 1, 75, 76, 84, 85, 115
Bartholomew 10
Bartolommeo, Fra 59
Basel/Ferrara, Council of (1431–1449) 31, 33, 45, 47
Basil of Ancyra 25
Basil the Great 9, 21, 24, 29, 30
Basilides 19
Bates, Joseph 107
Baur, F. C. 75, 84
Bavinck, Herman 85
Baxter, Richard 52, 63
Bede 31, 36, 42
Beecher, Henry Ward 102, 109
Beecher, Lyman 95, 102, 104, 109
Beghards 47
Beguines 47
Beissel, Conrad 97
Belgic Confession 67
Bell, L. Nelson 86
Bellarmine, Robert 54, 68
Benedict XII 42
Benedict XIII 47
Benedict of Nursia 1, 29, 31, 42
Benedictines 29, 31, 36, 42, 43
Bengel, J. A. 75, 80
Bennett, Dennis 116, 117
Berg, Carolina Sandell 8
Berkeley, George 78
Berkeley, John 96
Berkhof, Louis 95, 115
Bernard of Clairvaux 1, 8, 31, 38, 40, 42, 43
Bernard of Cluny 8
Berthold 42
Beza, Theodore 50, 56, 57, 67
Birgitta 43
Bishop, Ervin 92
Blackstone, William E. 95, 111
Blair, Samuel 94, 99
Blanchard, Jonathan 104

195